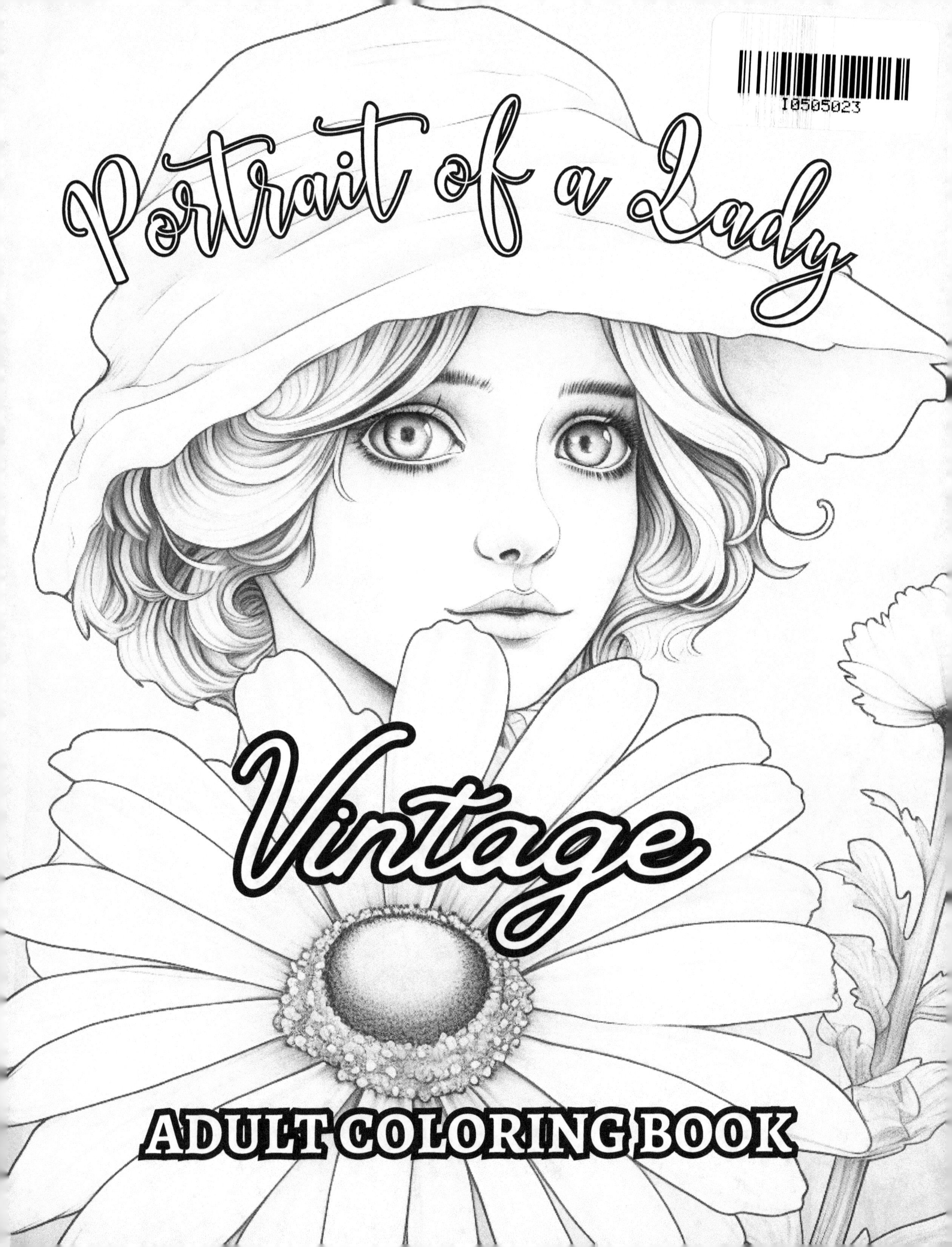
Portrait of a Lady
Vintage
ADULT COLORING BOOK

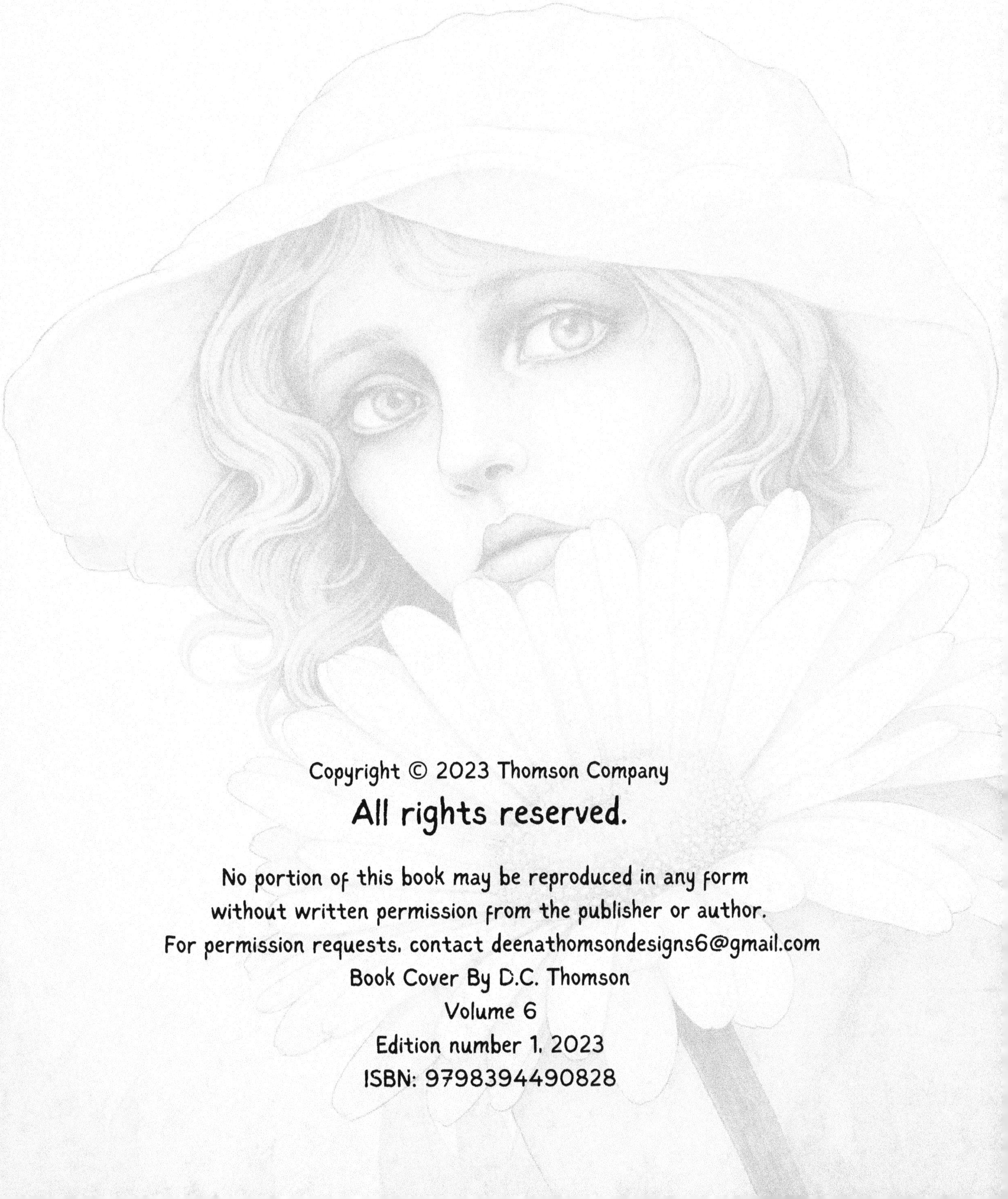

Book Cover By D.C. Thomson

Volume 6

Edition number 1, 2023

ISBN: 9798394490828

[illegible] number [illegible] 22[illegible]

ISBN [illegible]

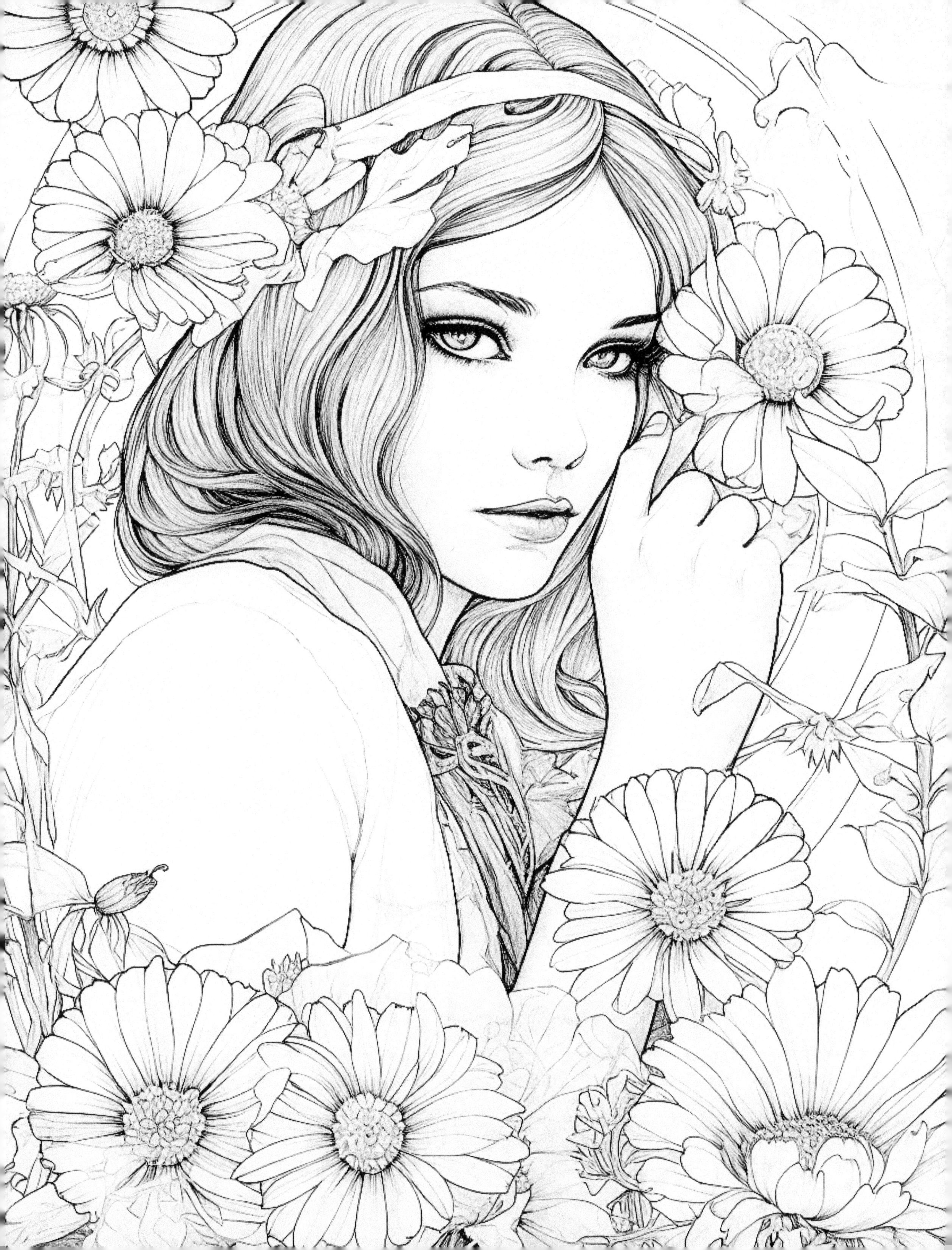

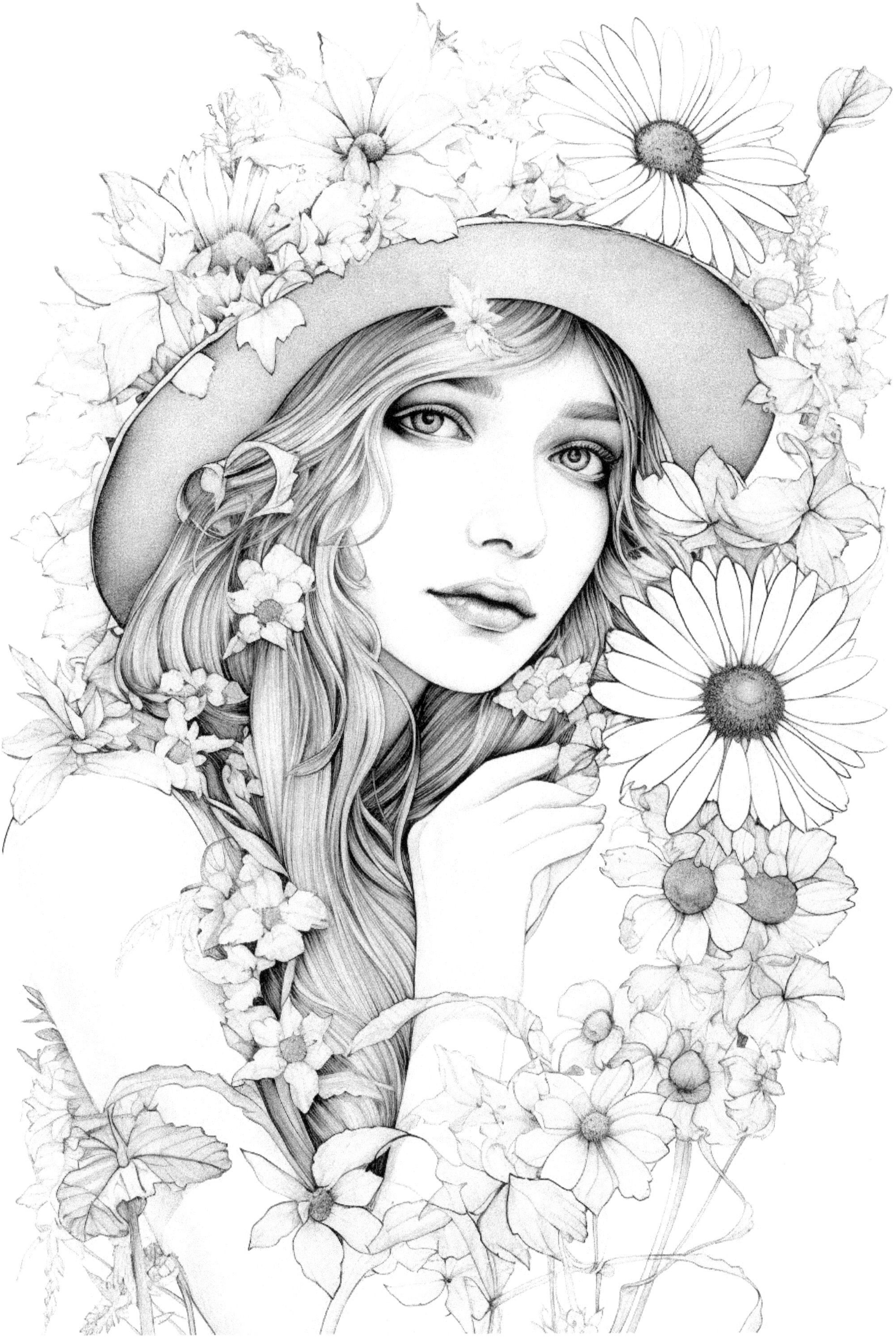

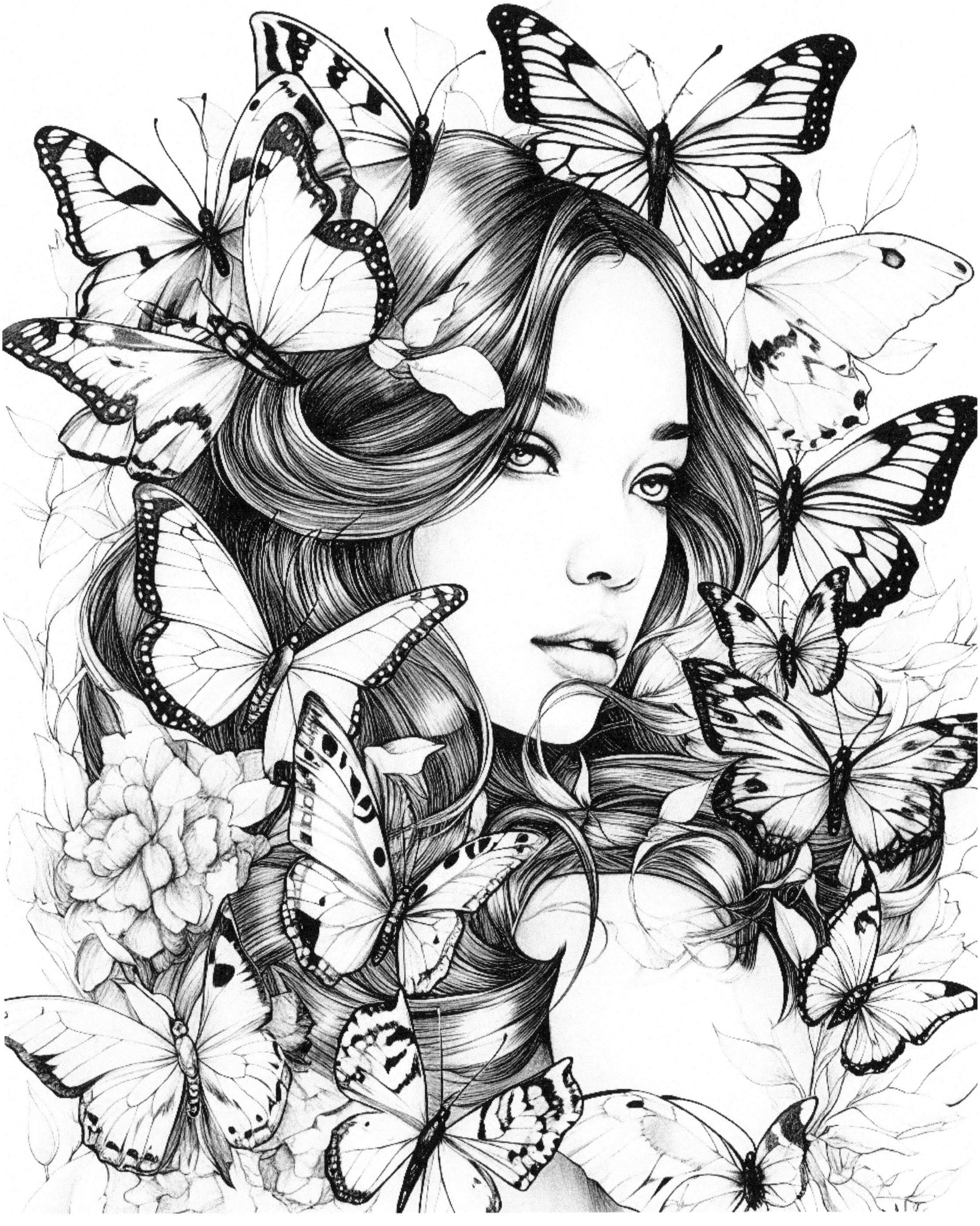

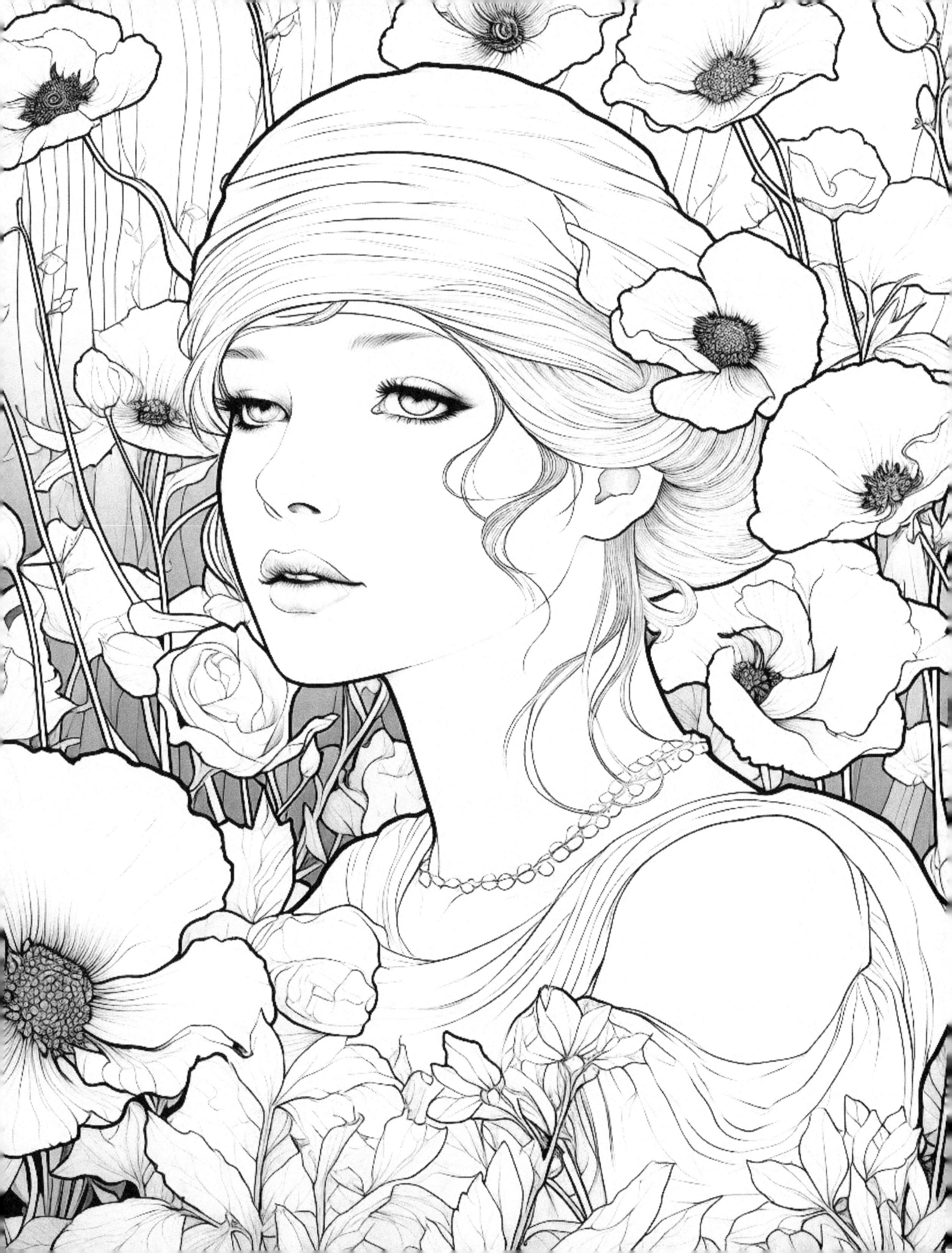

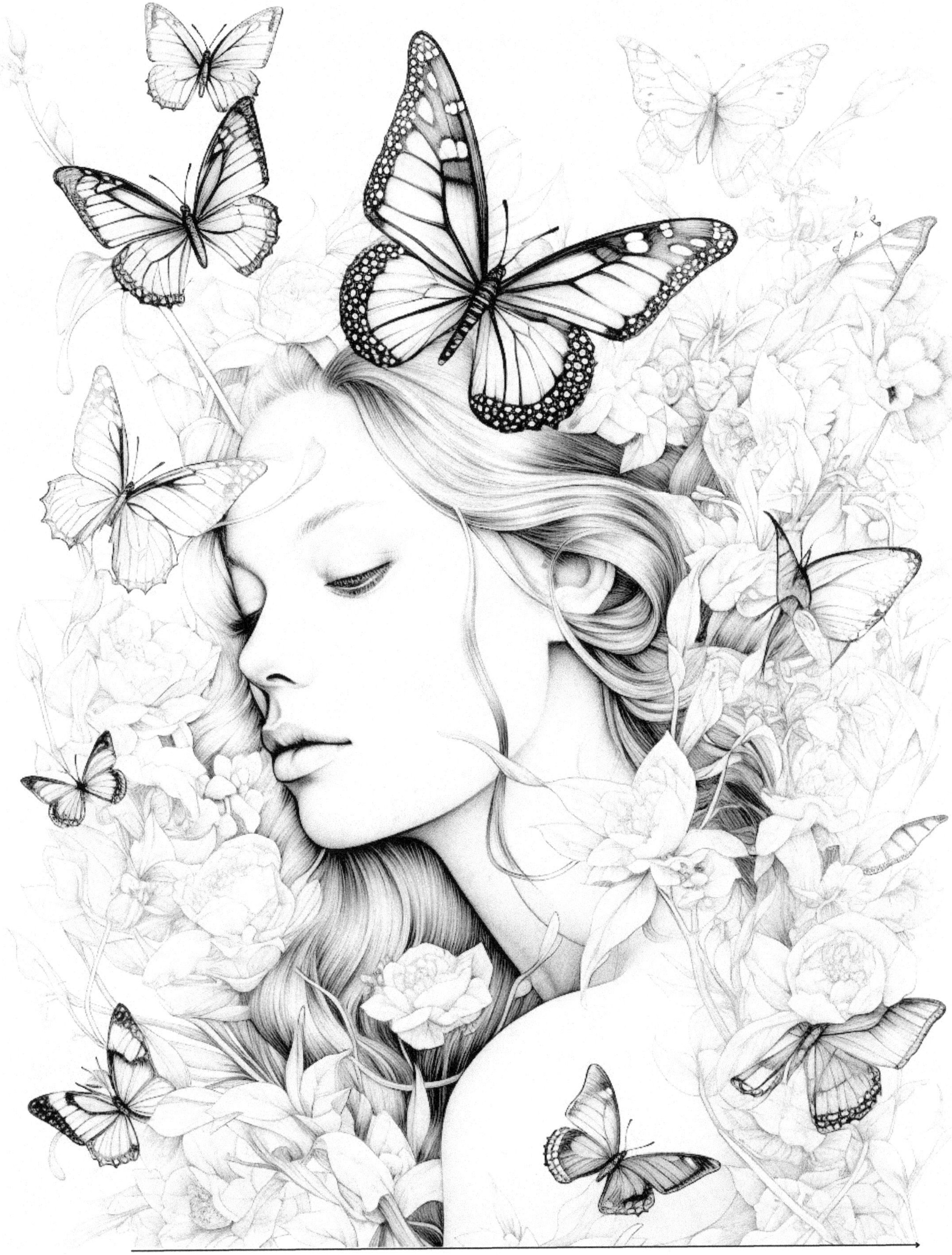

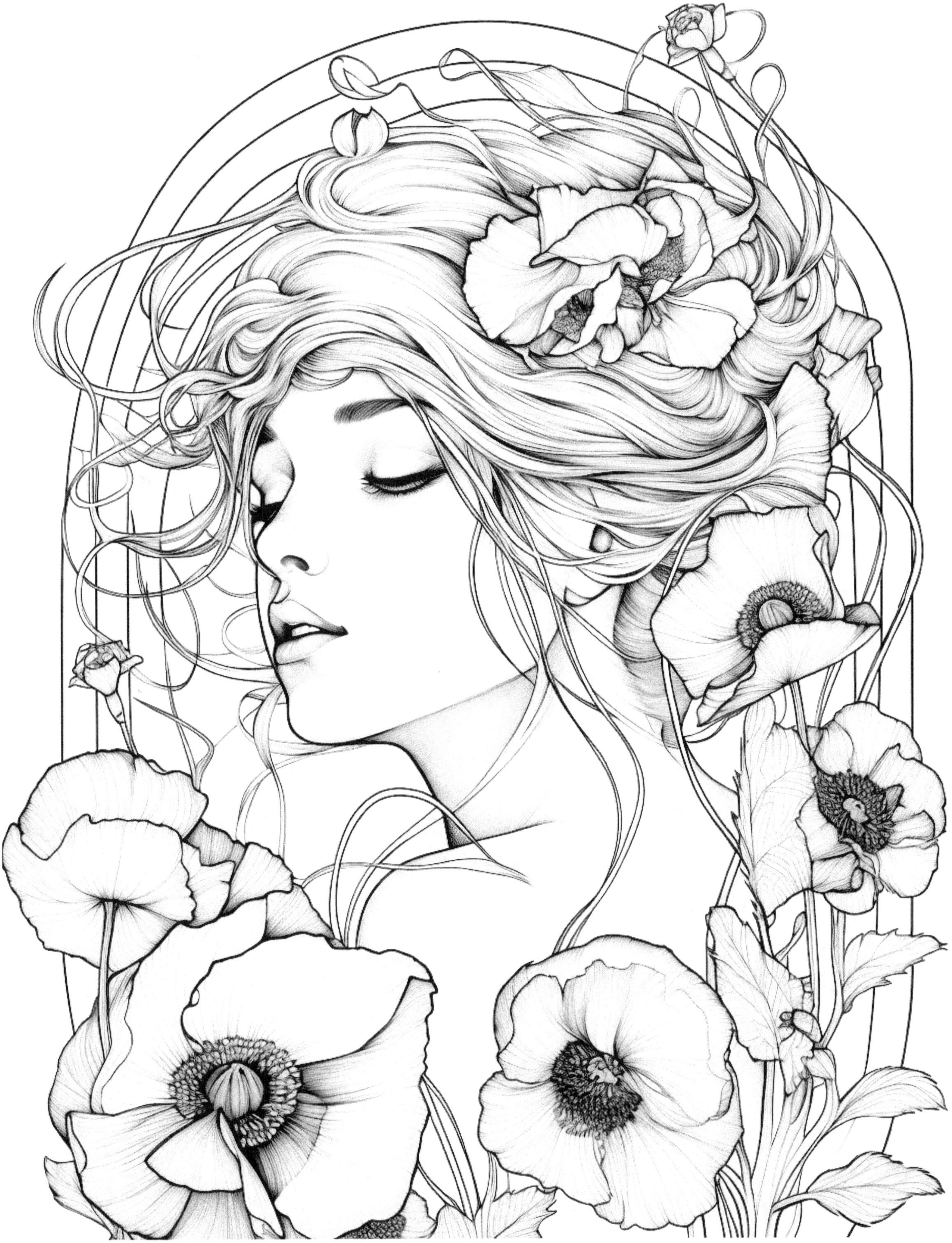

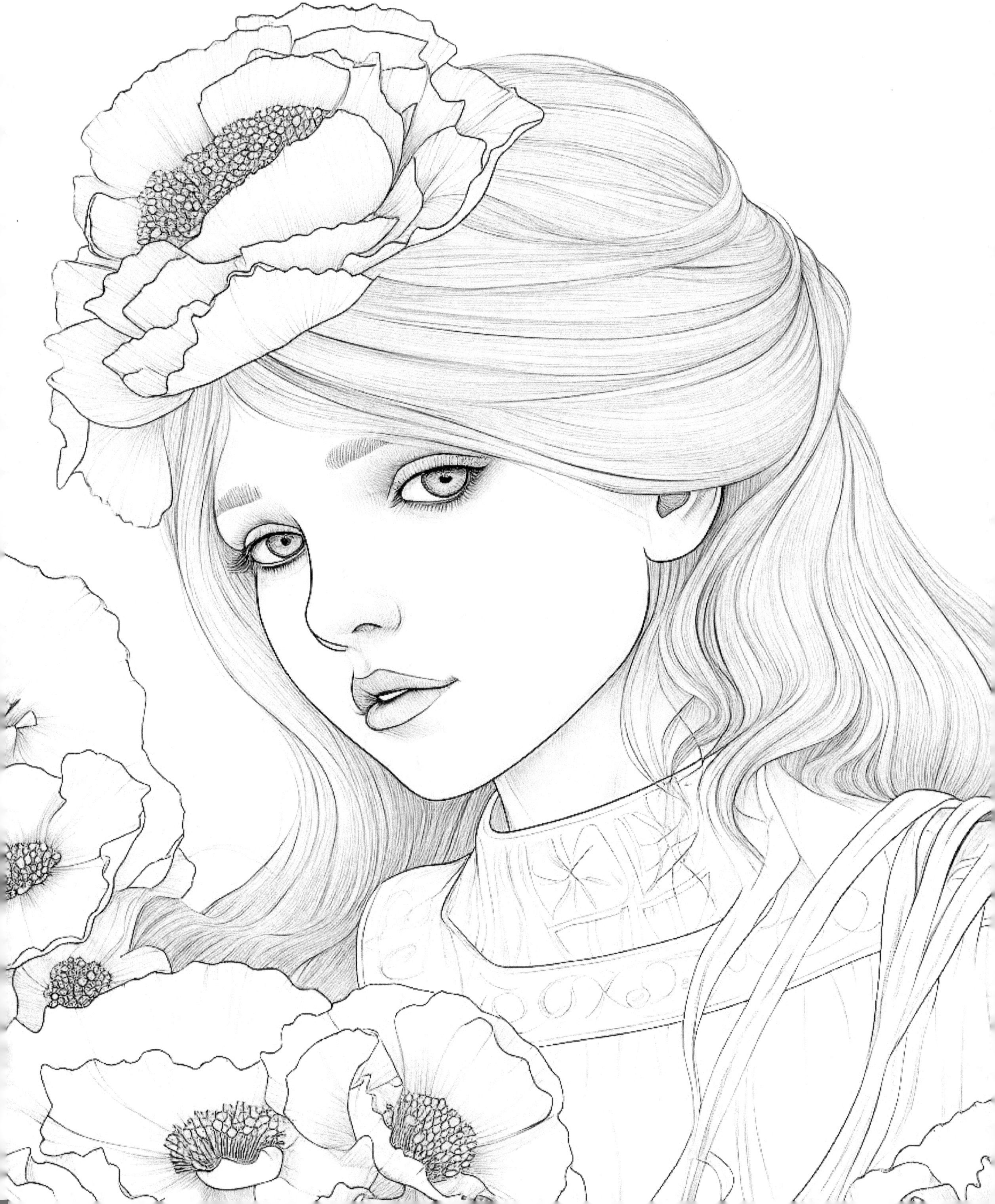

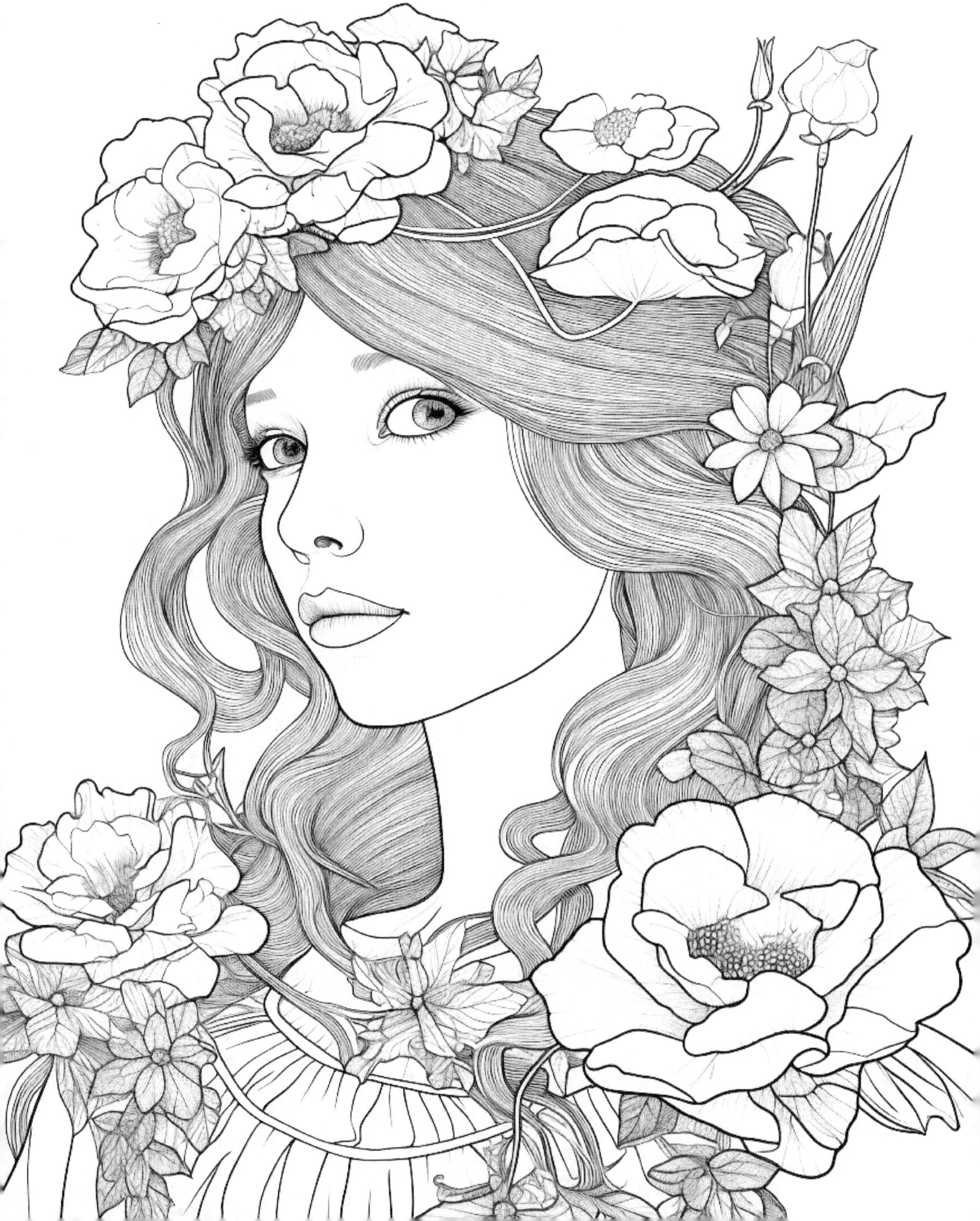

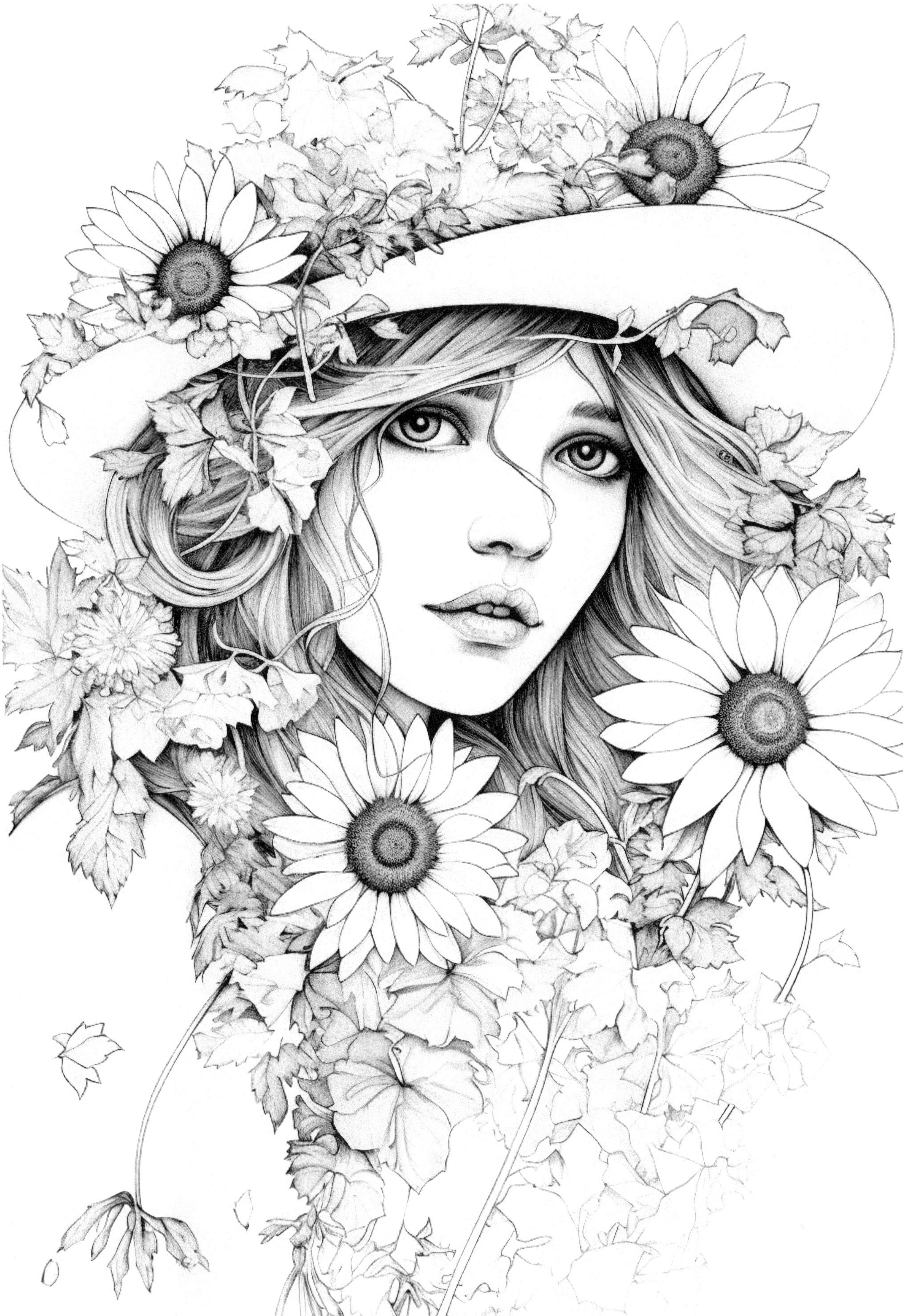

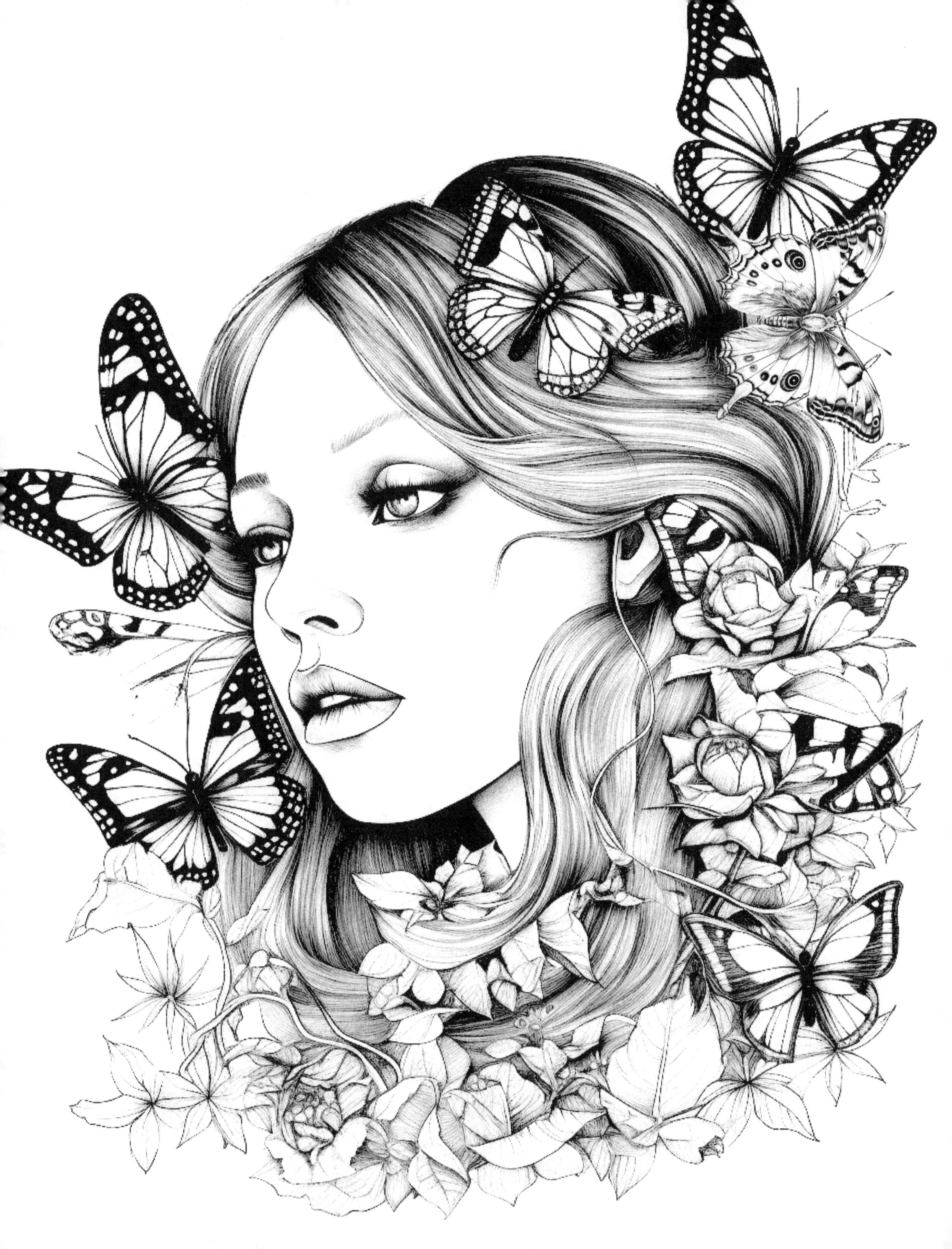

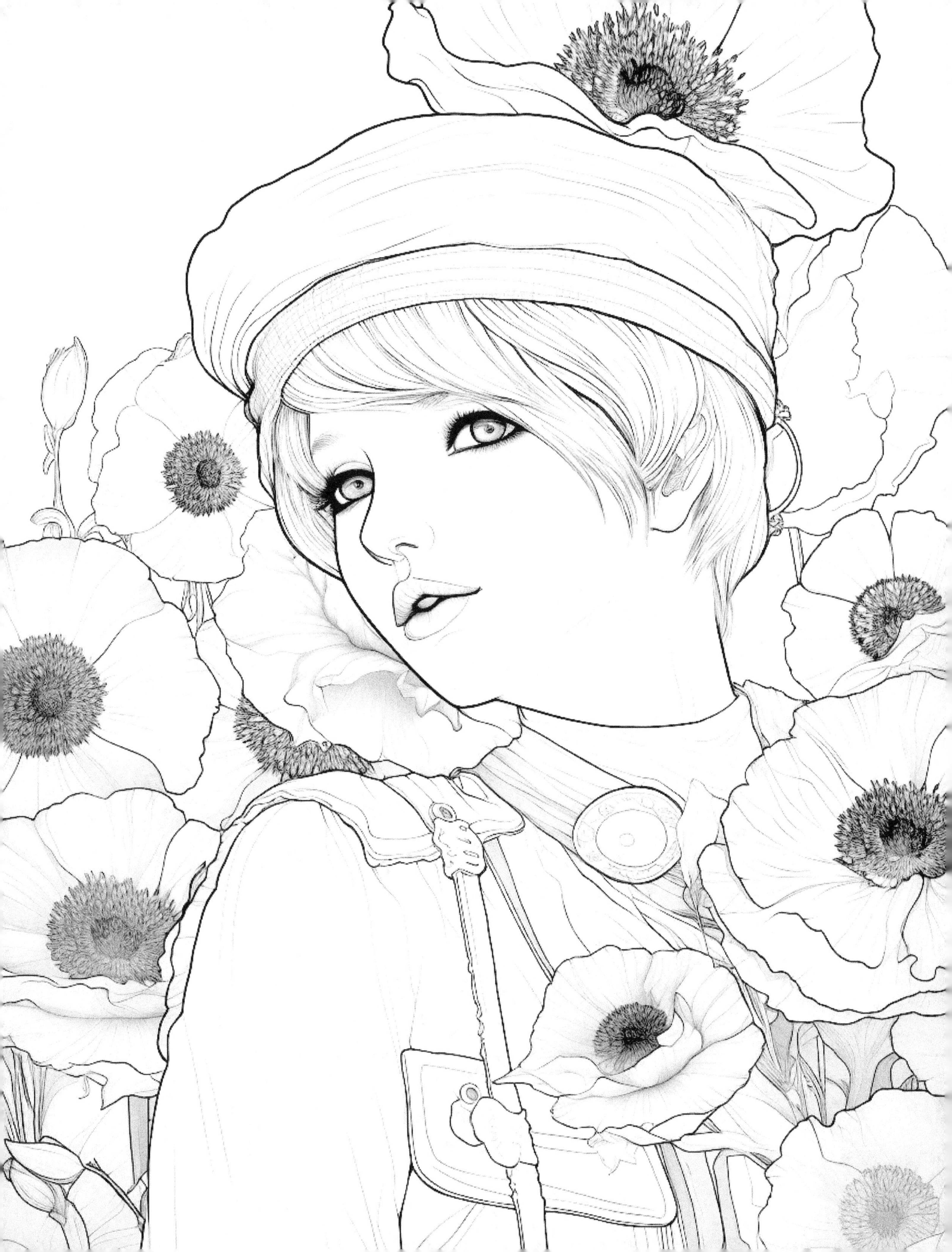

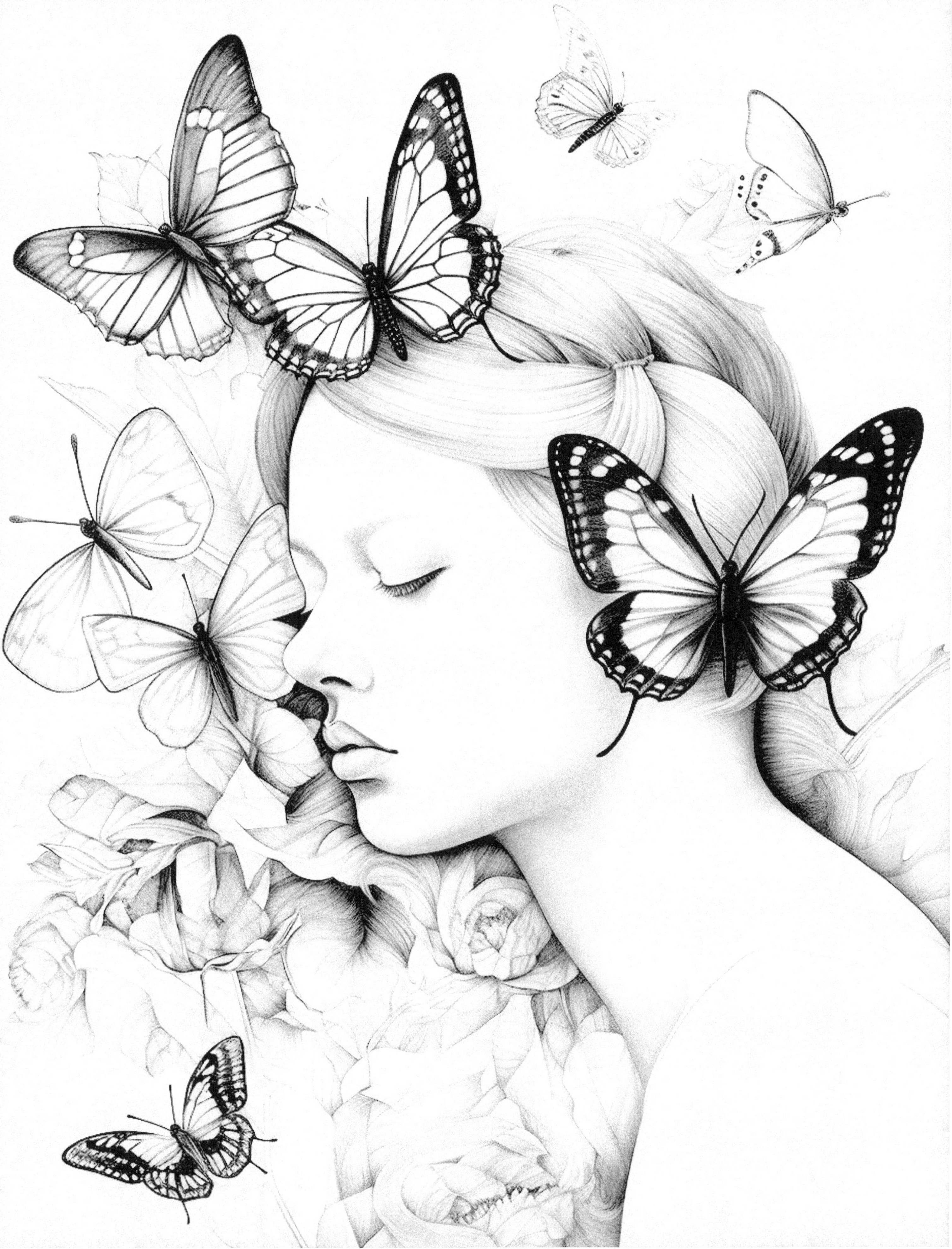

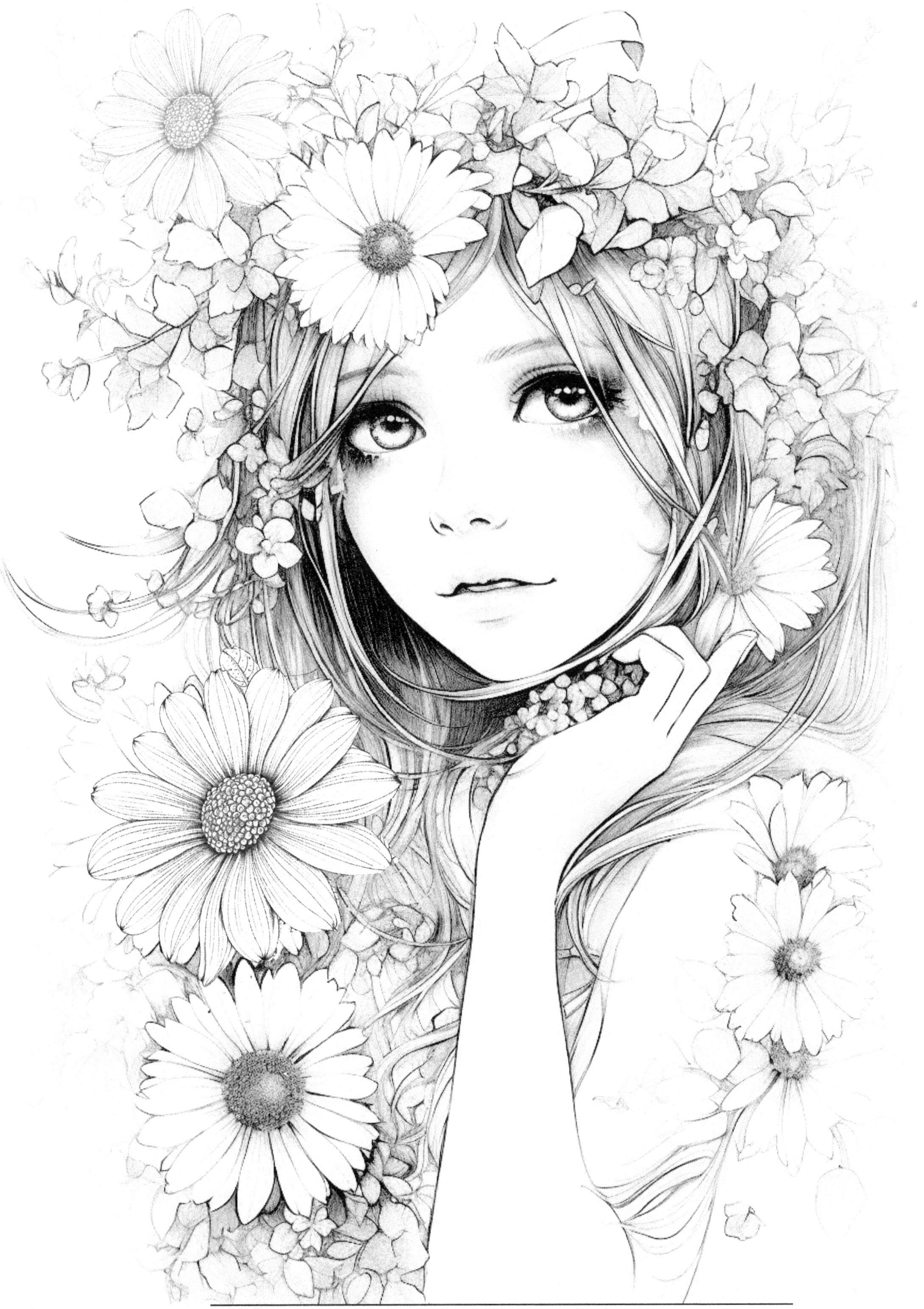

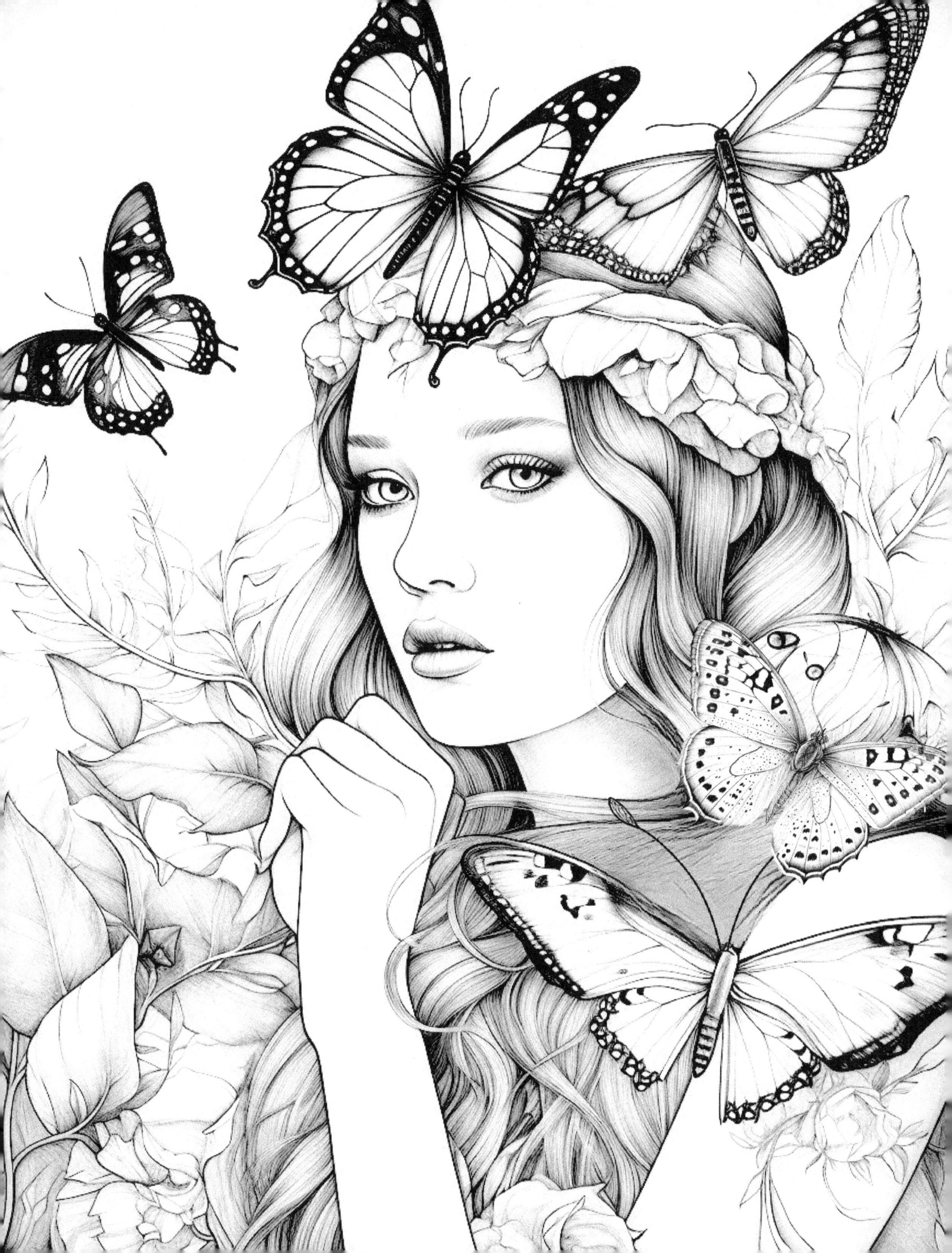

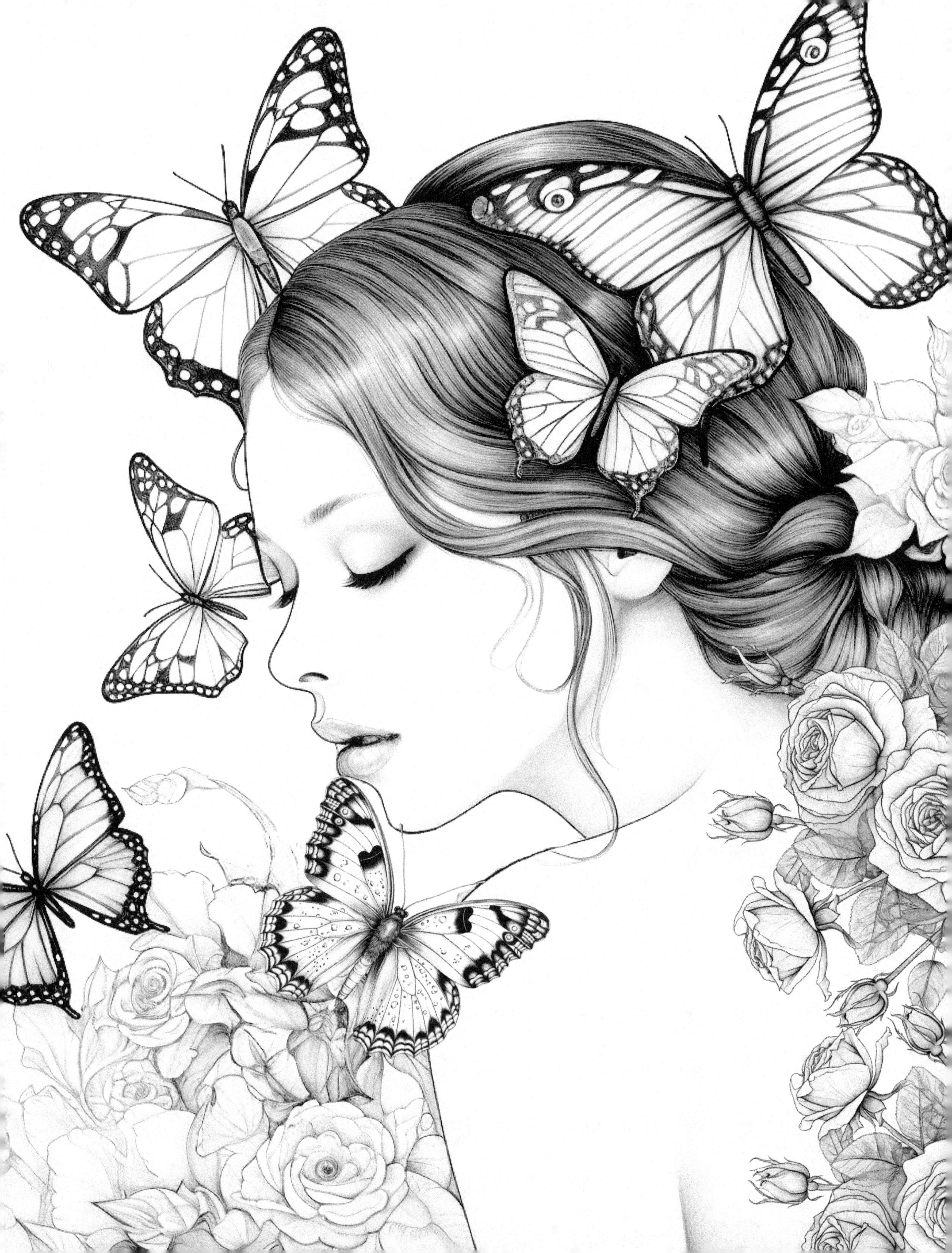

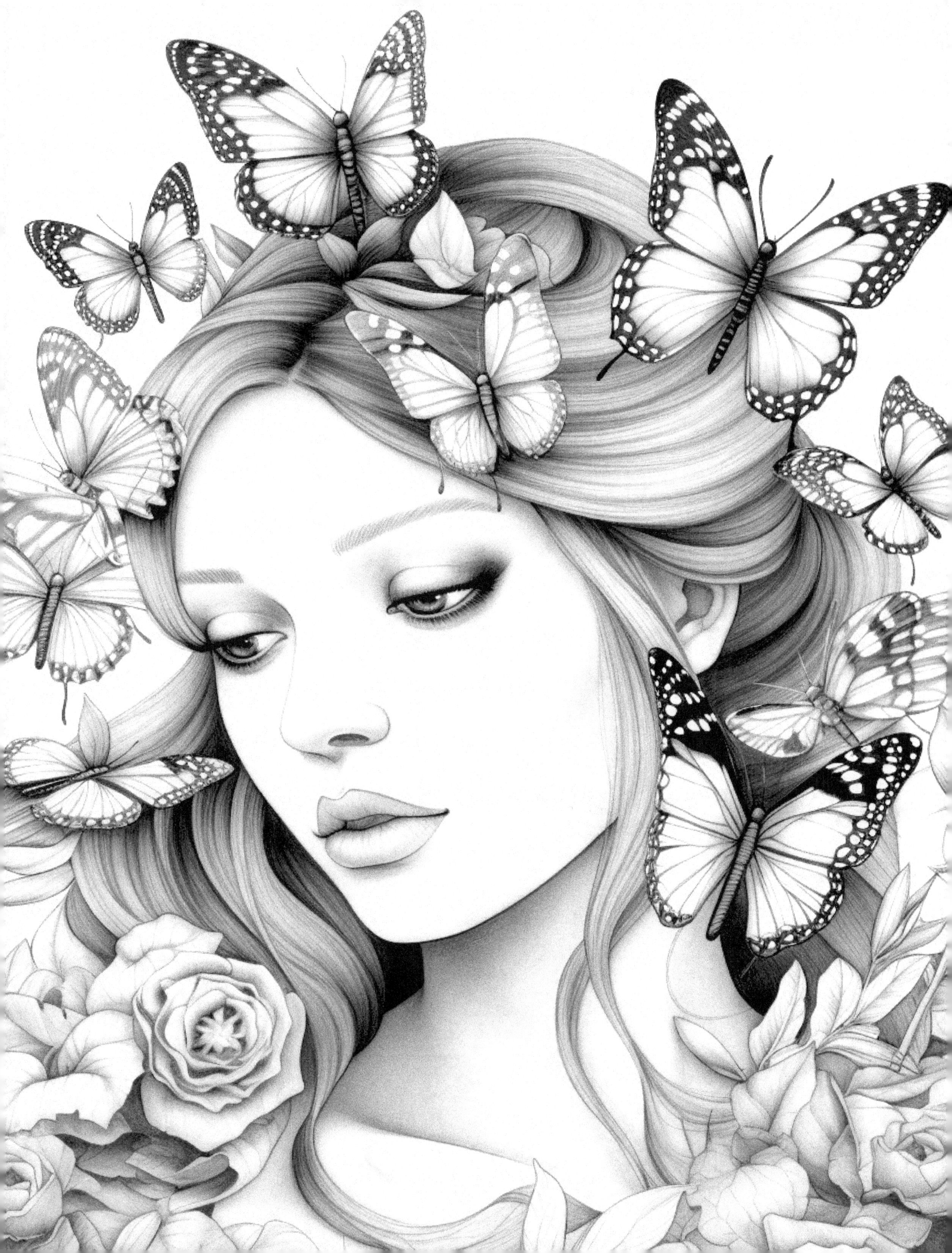

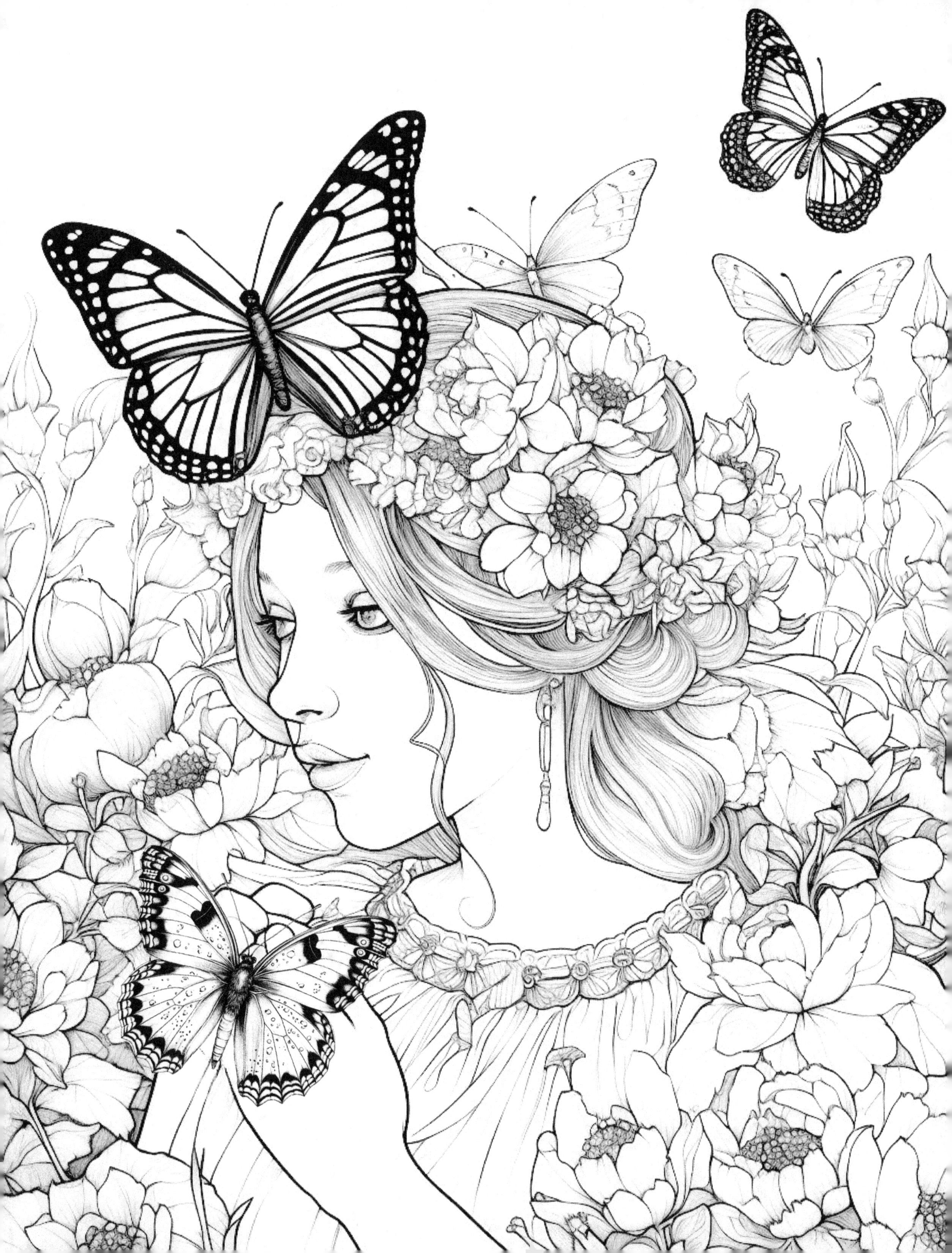

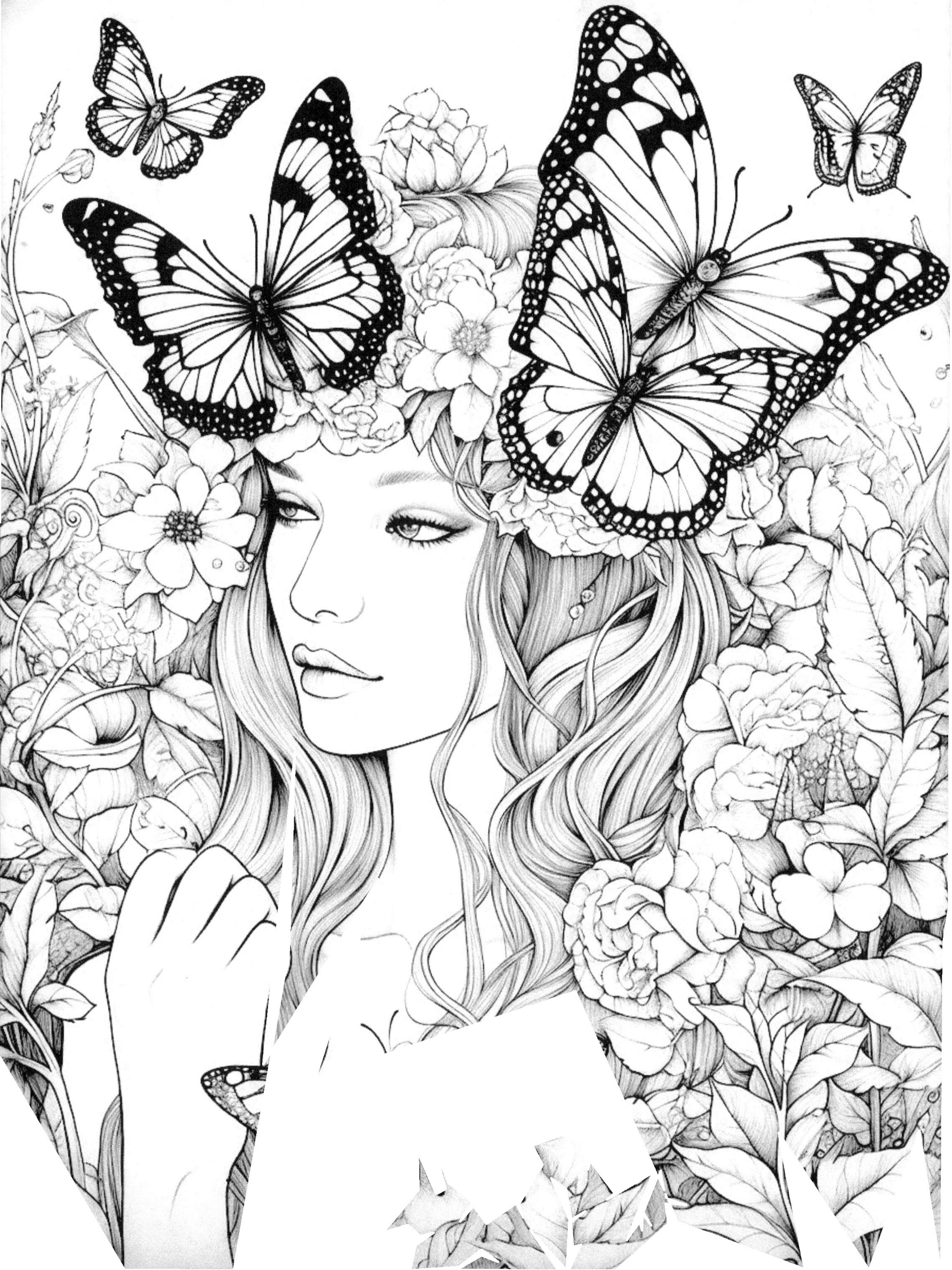

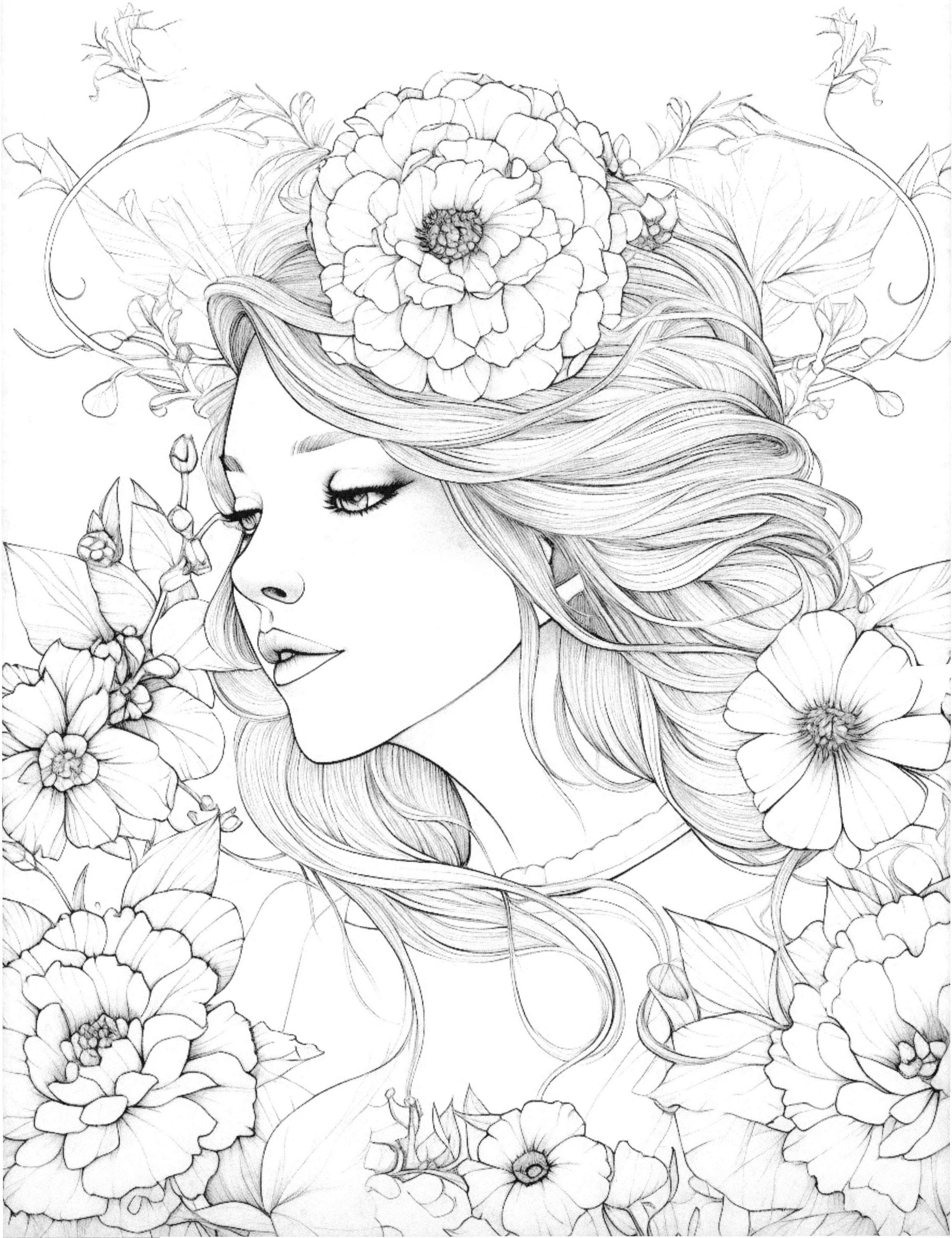

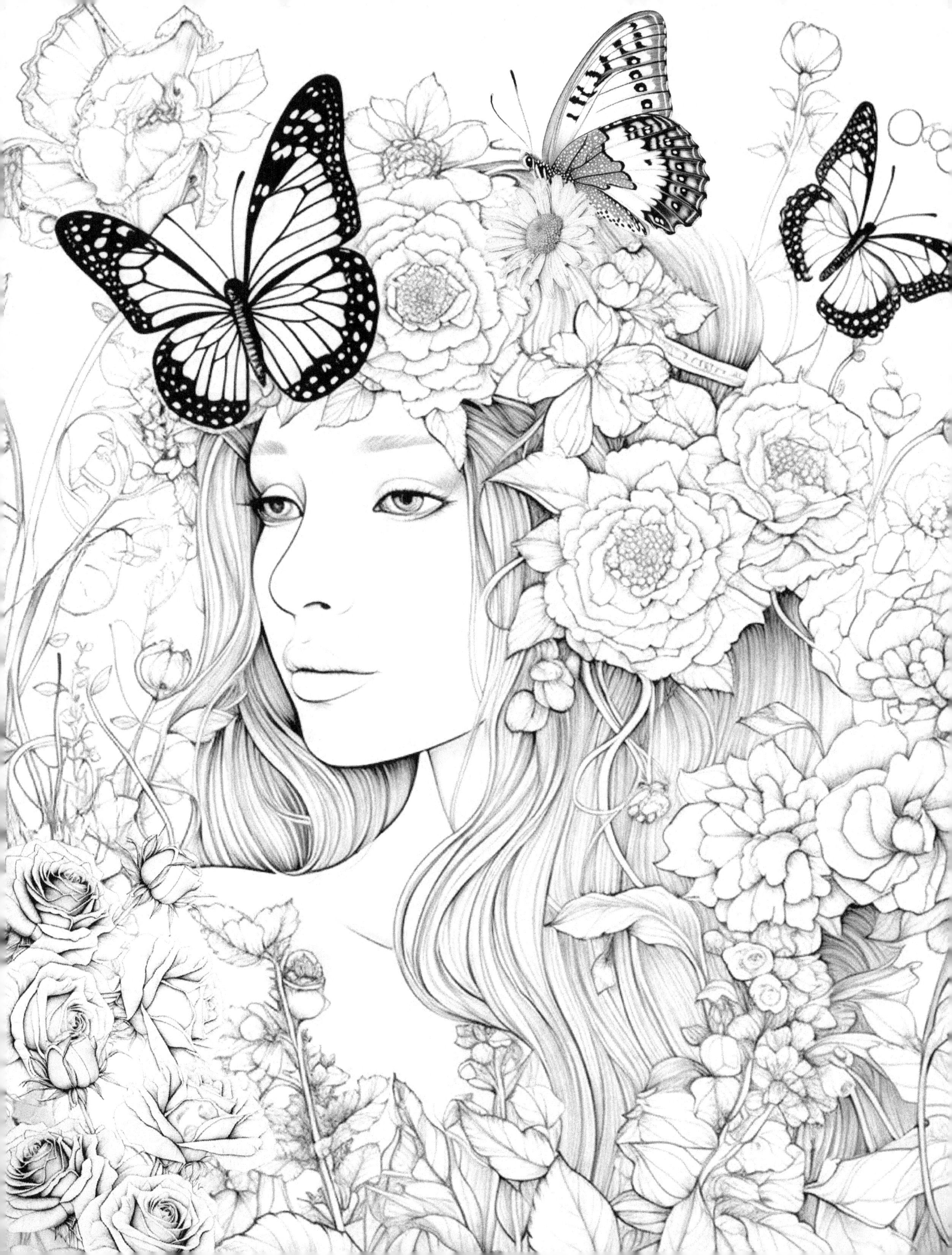

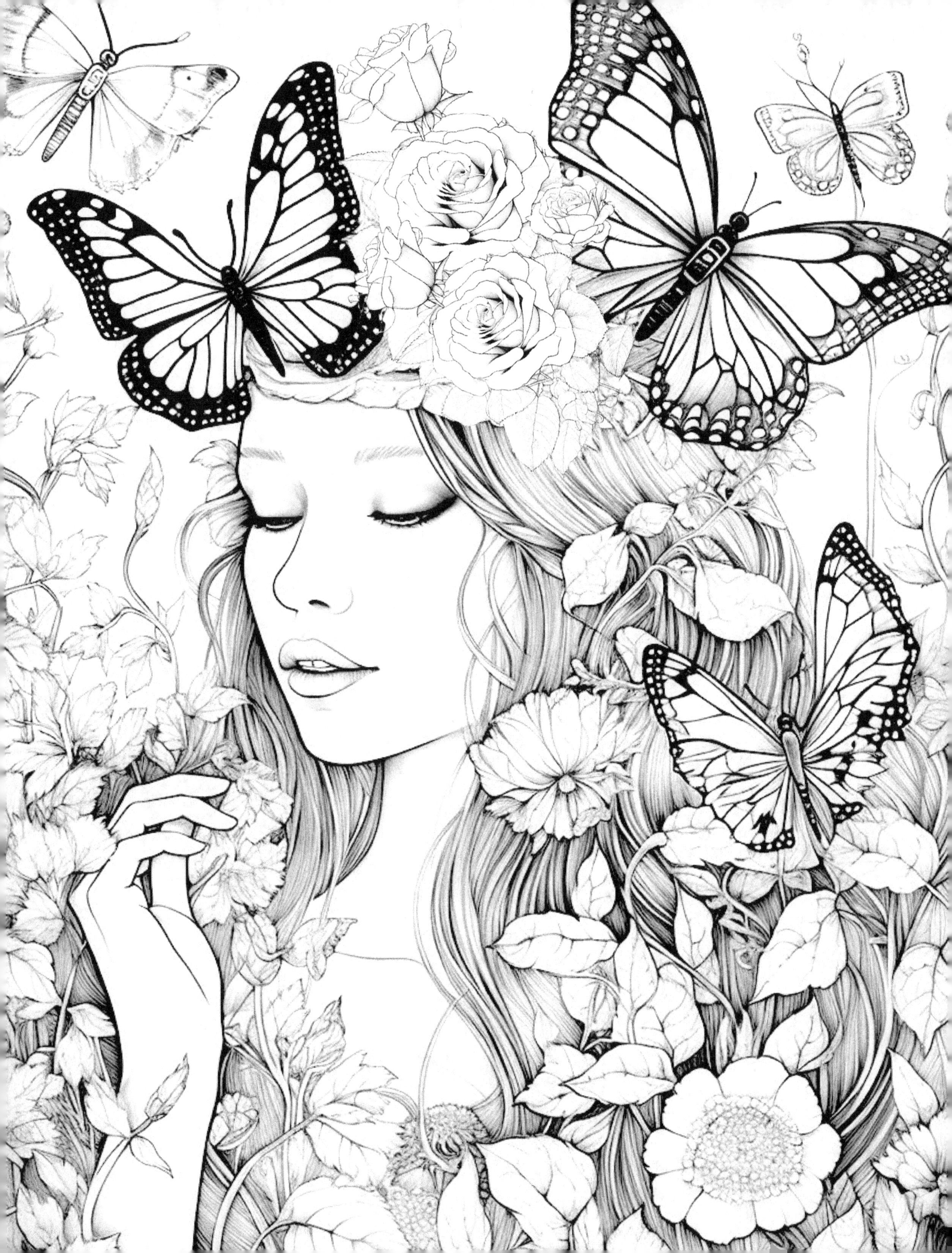

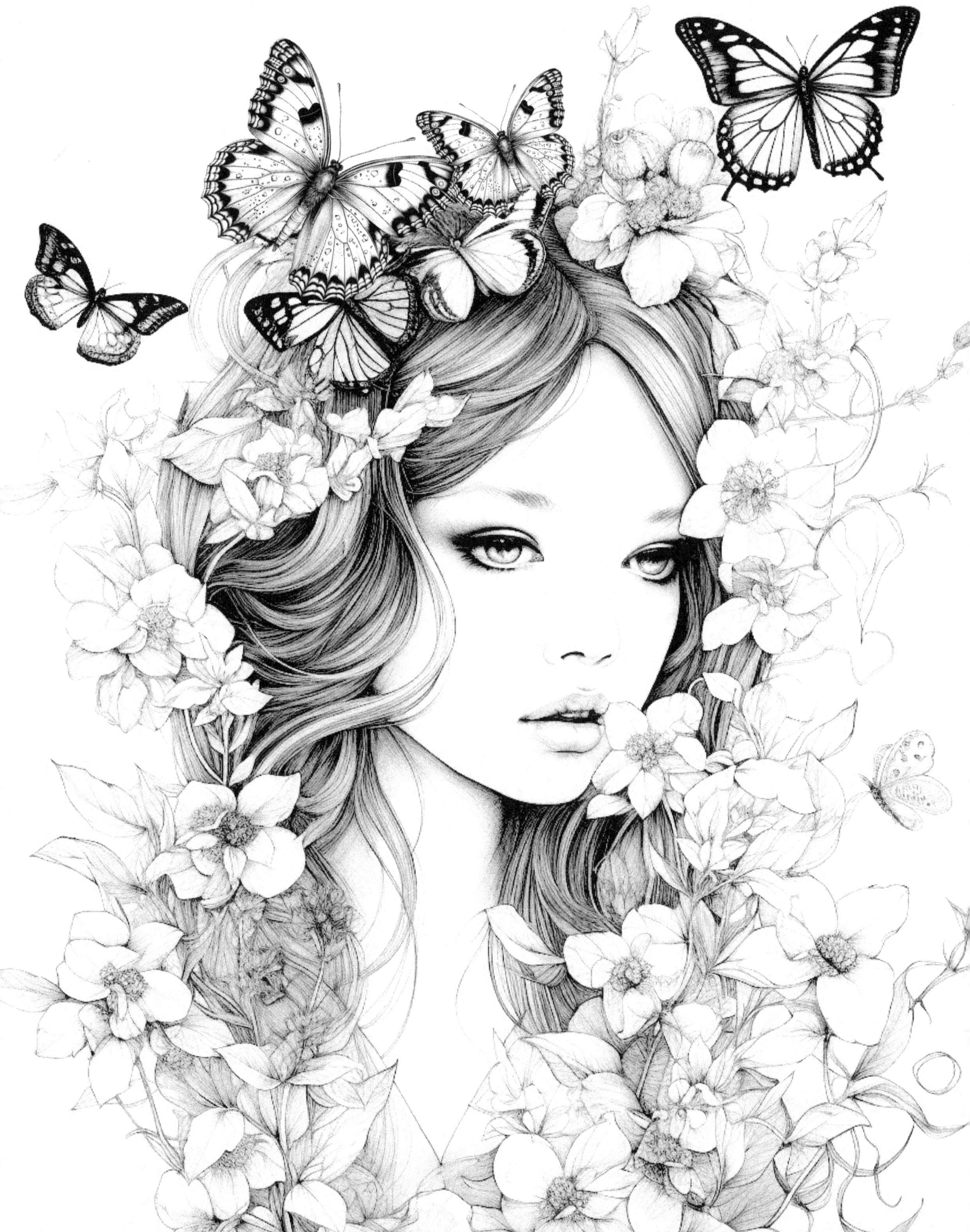

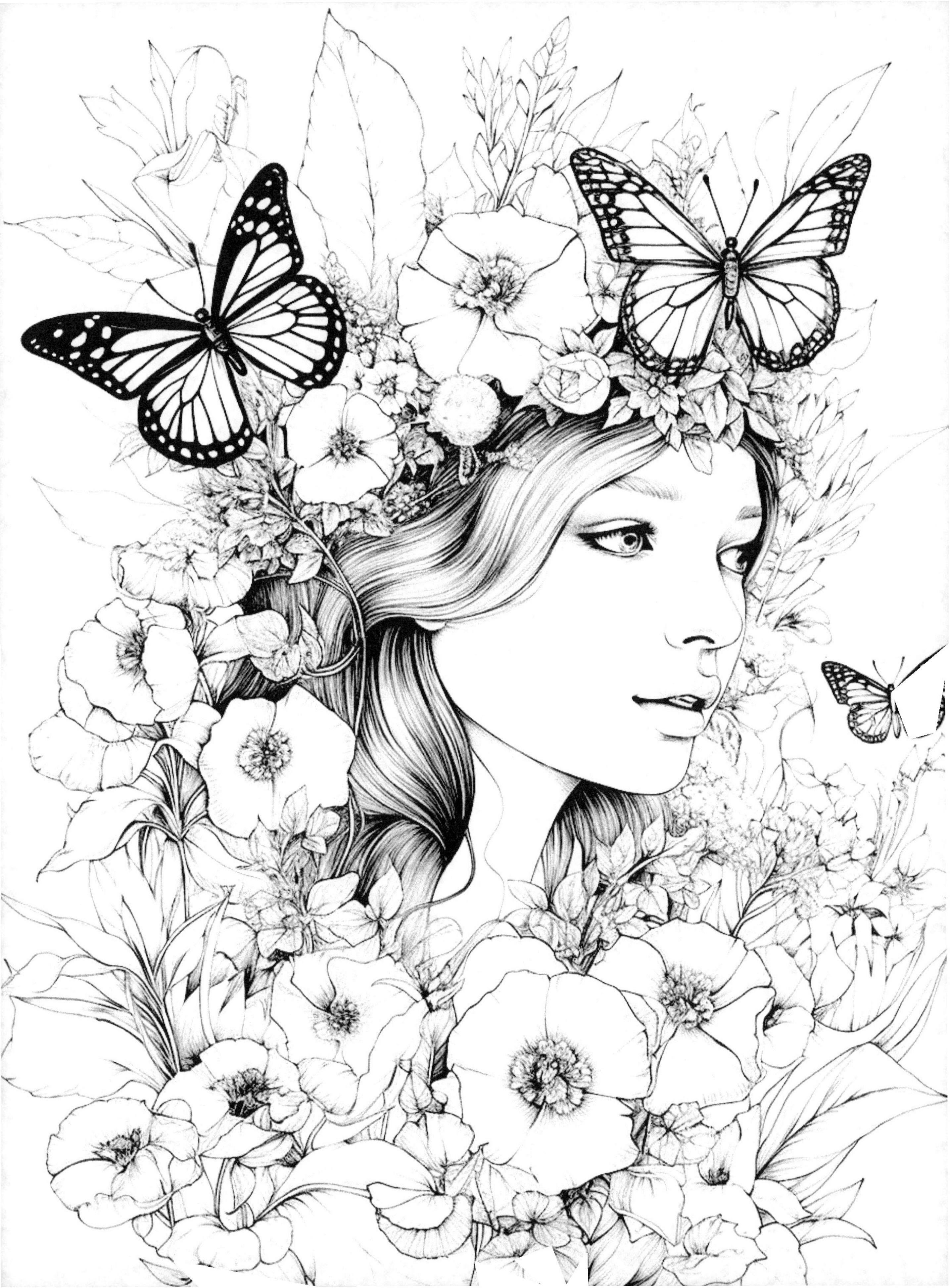

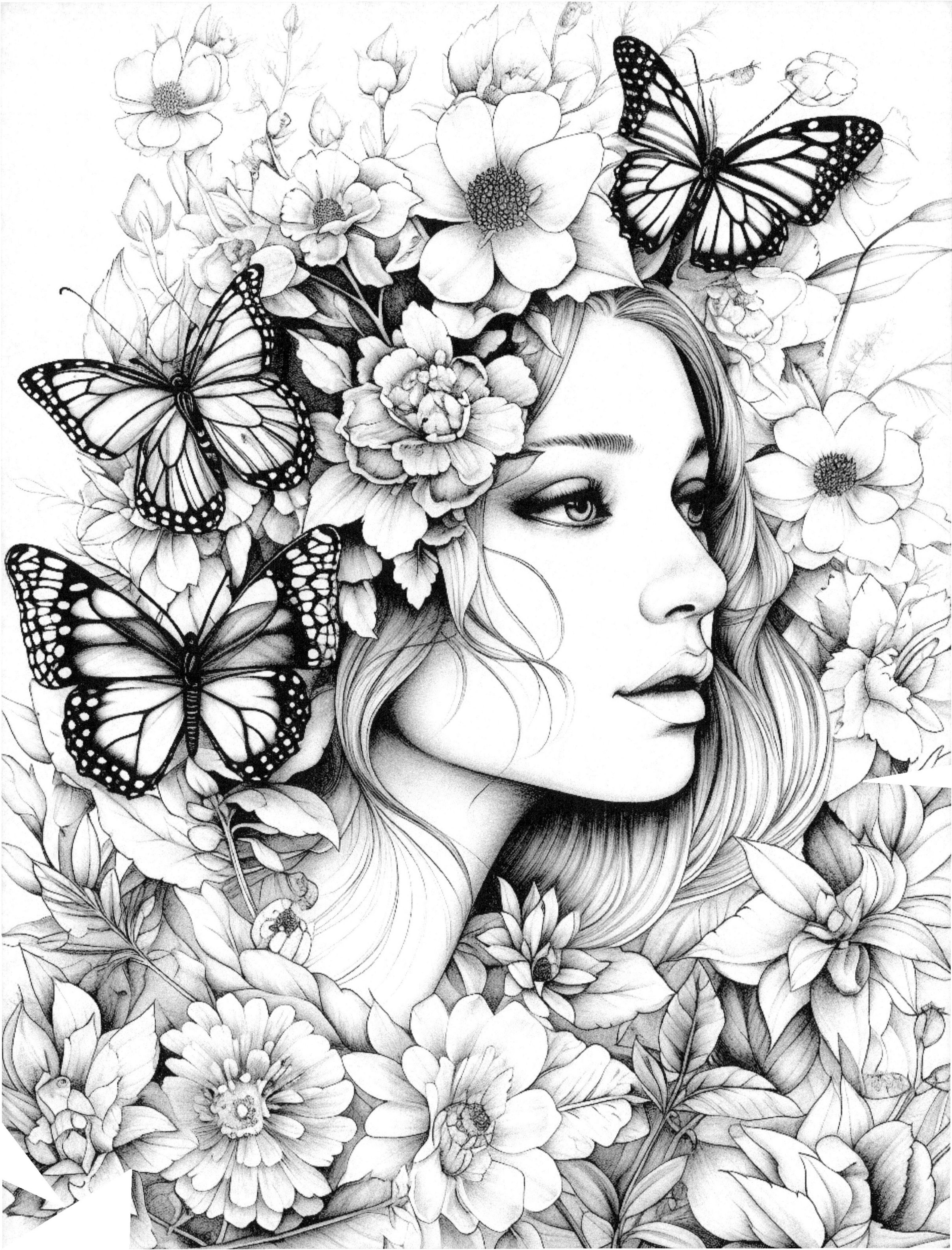

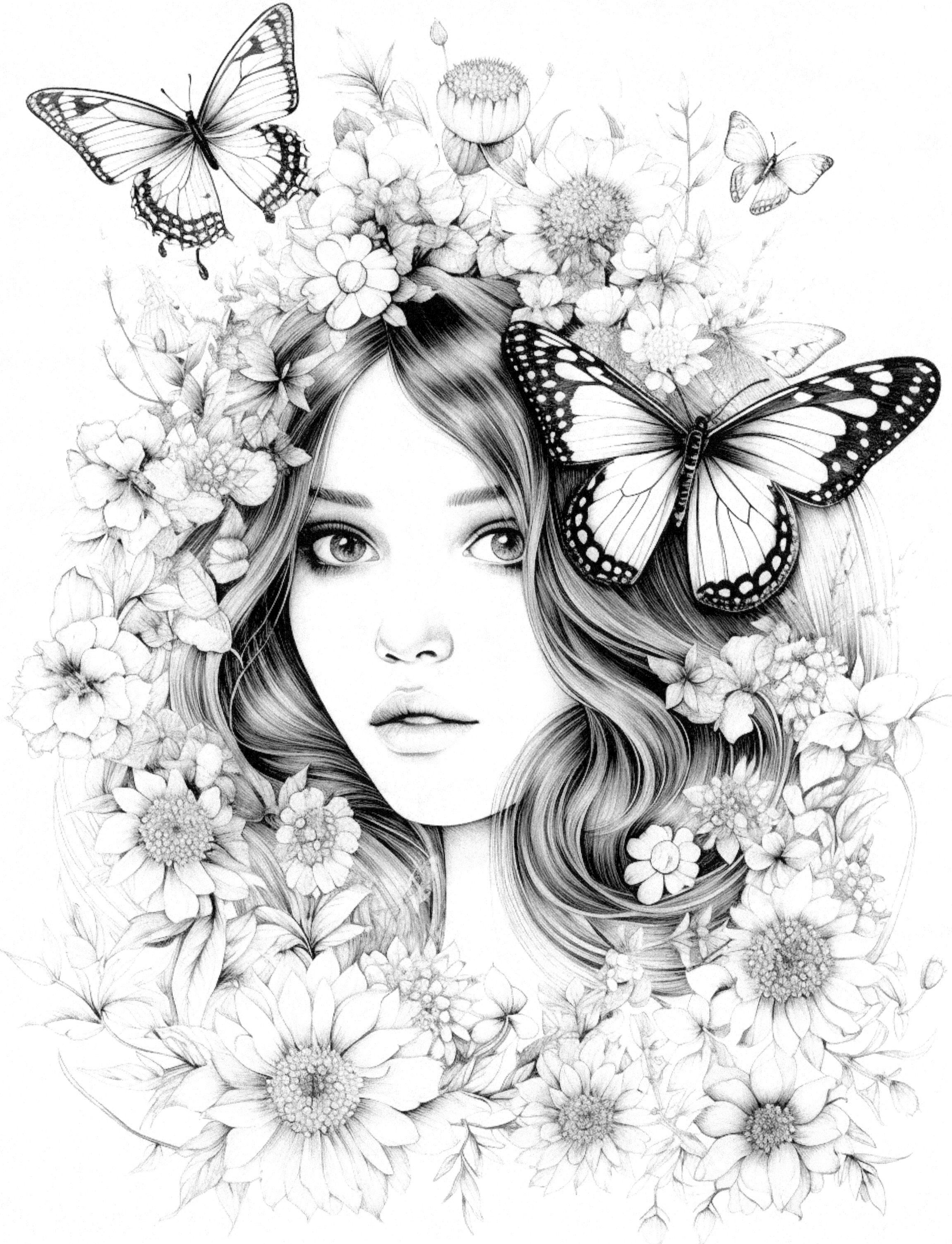

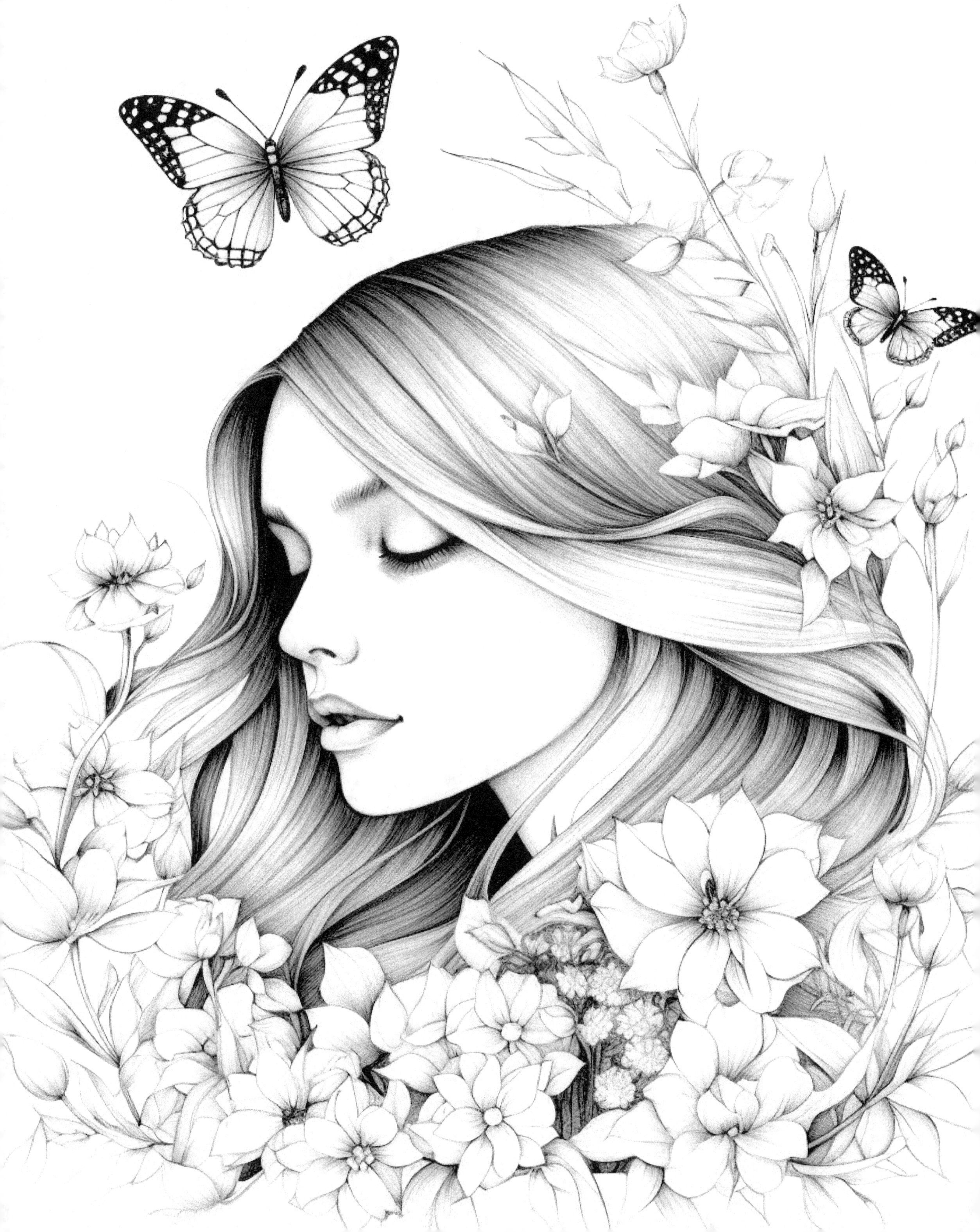

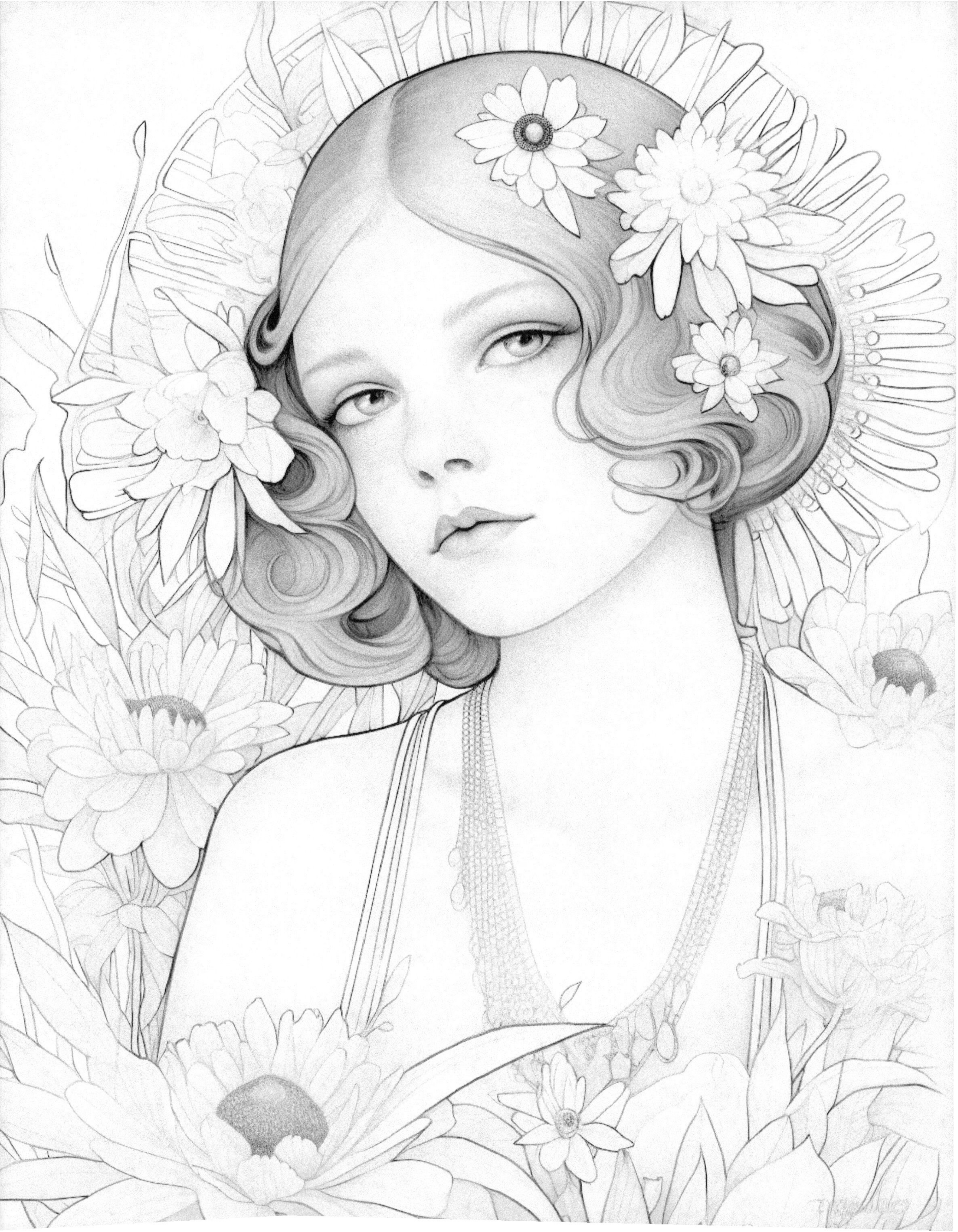

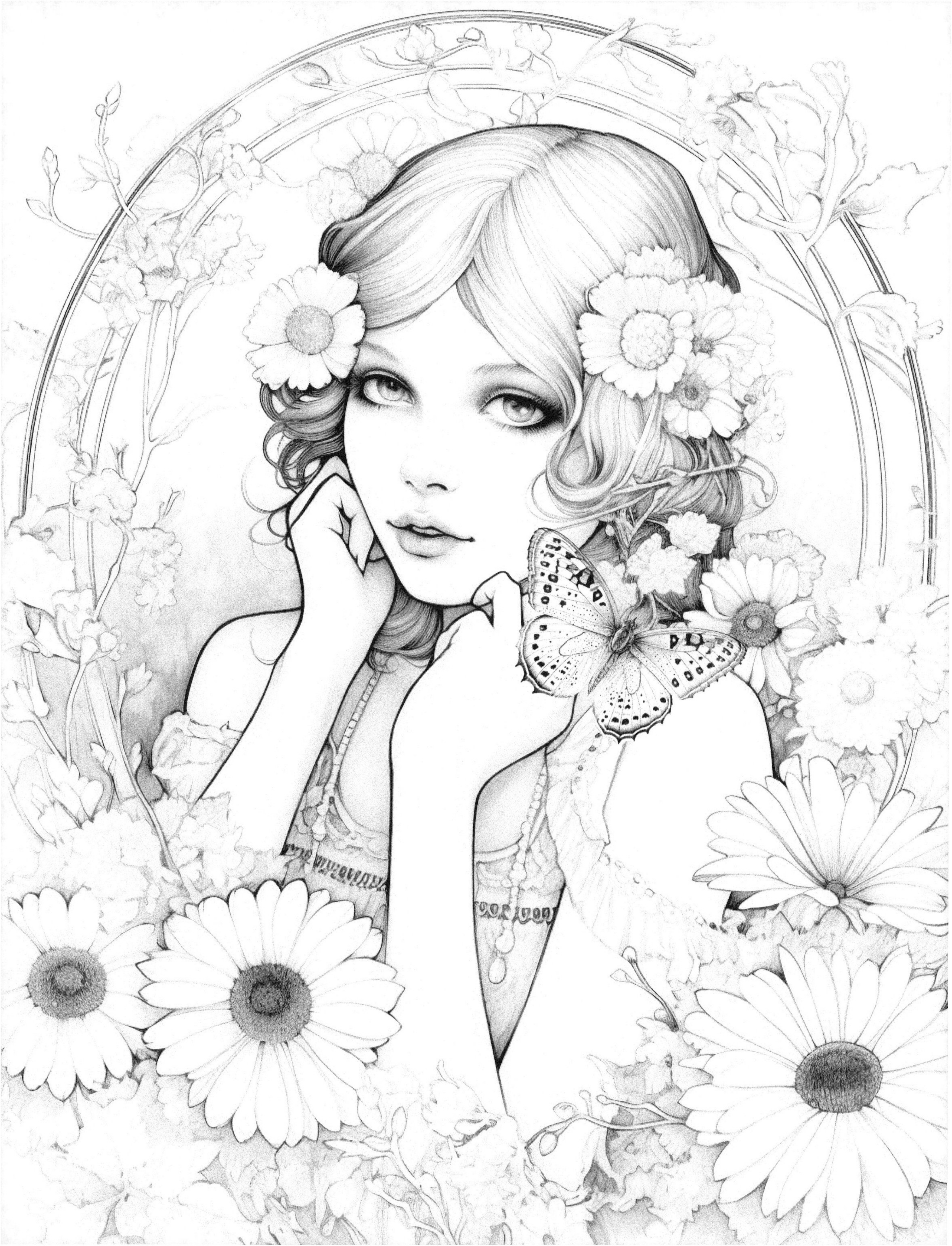

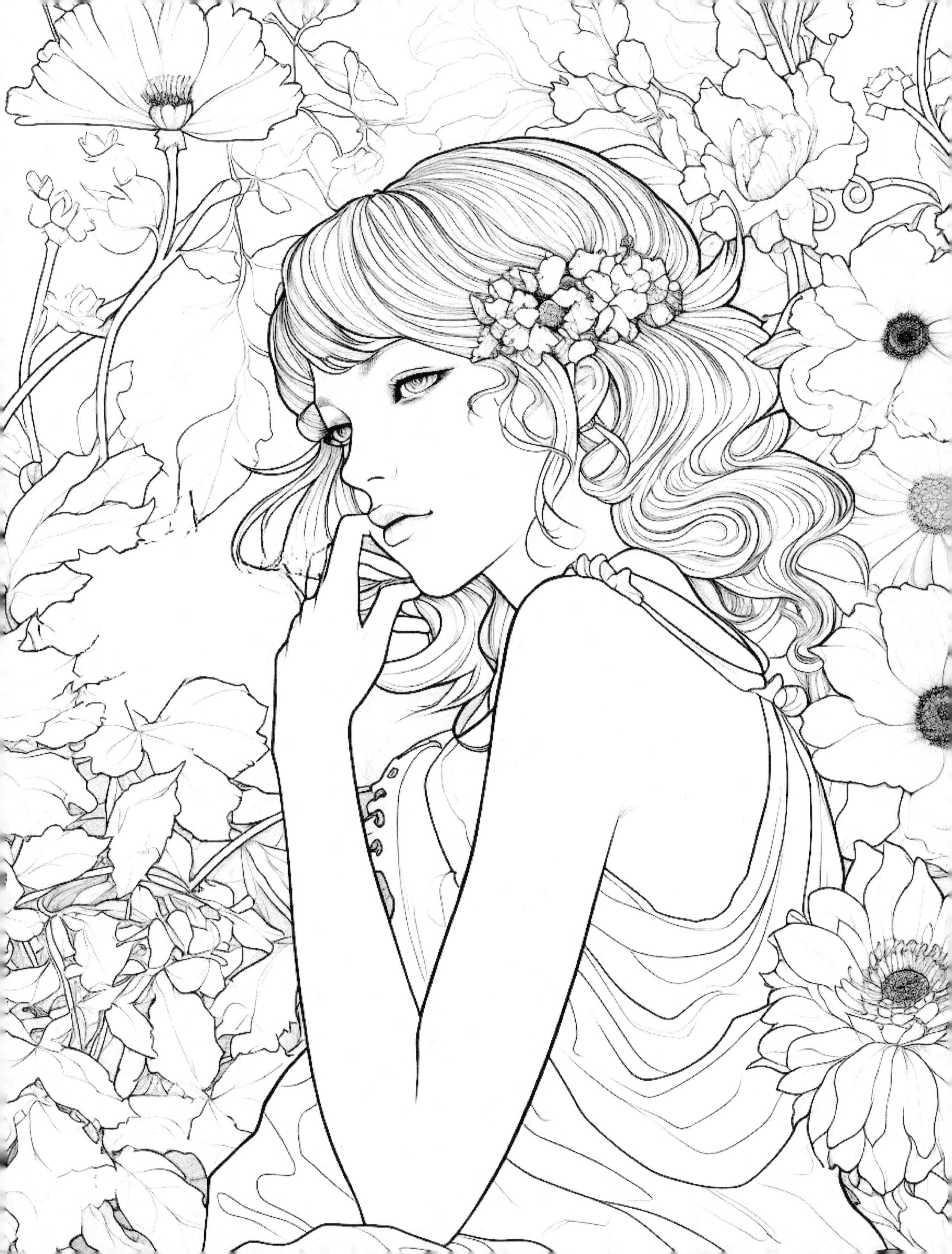

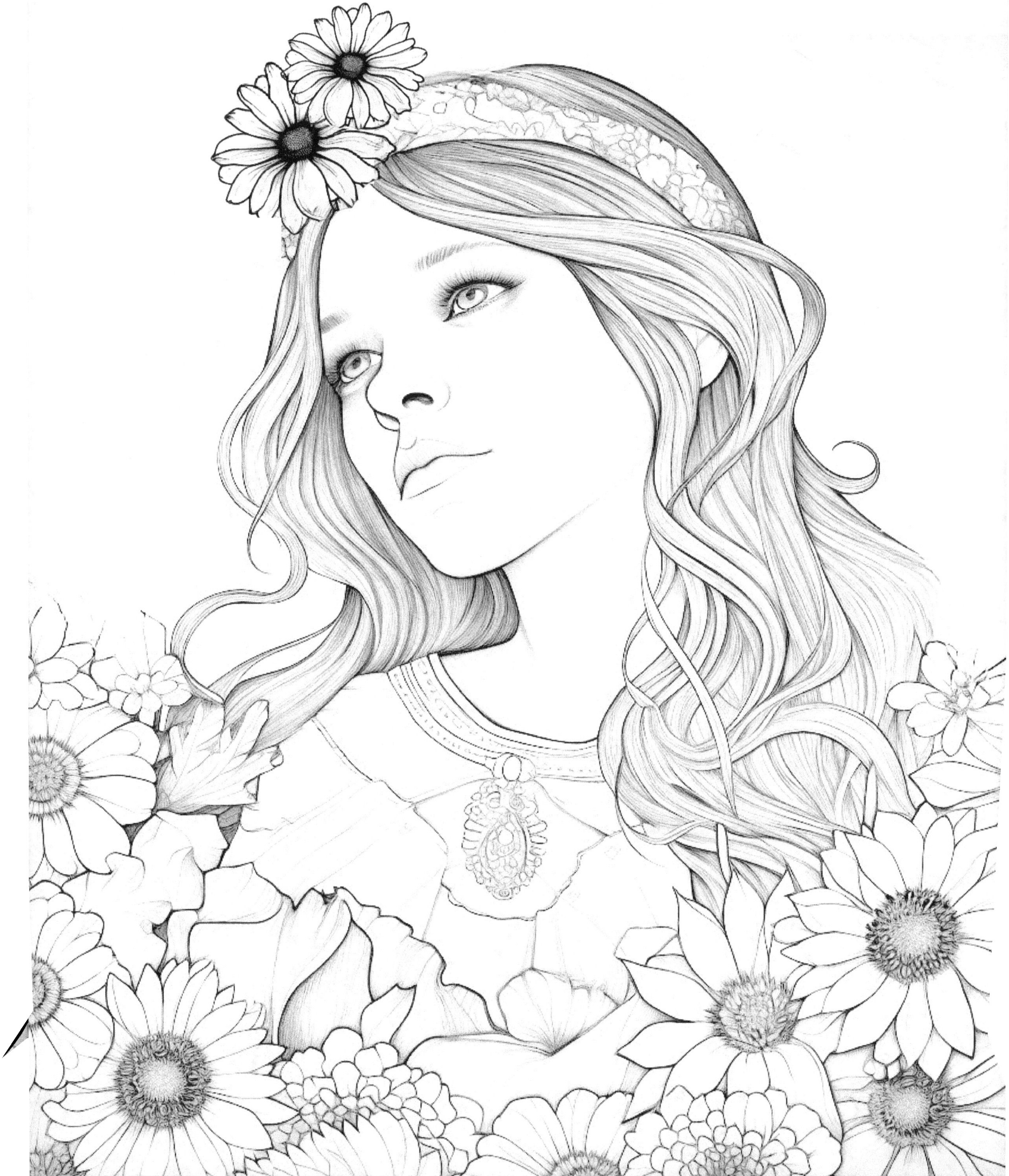

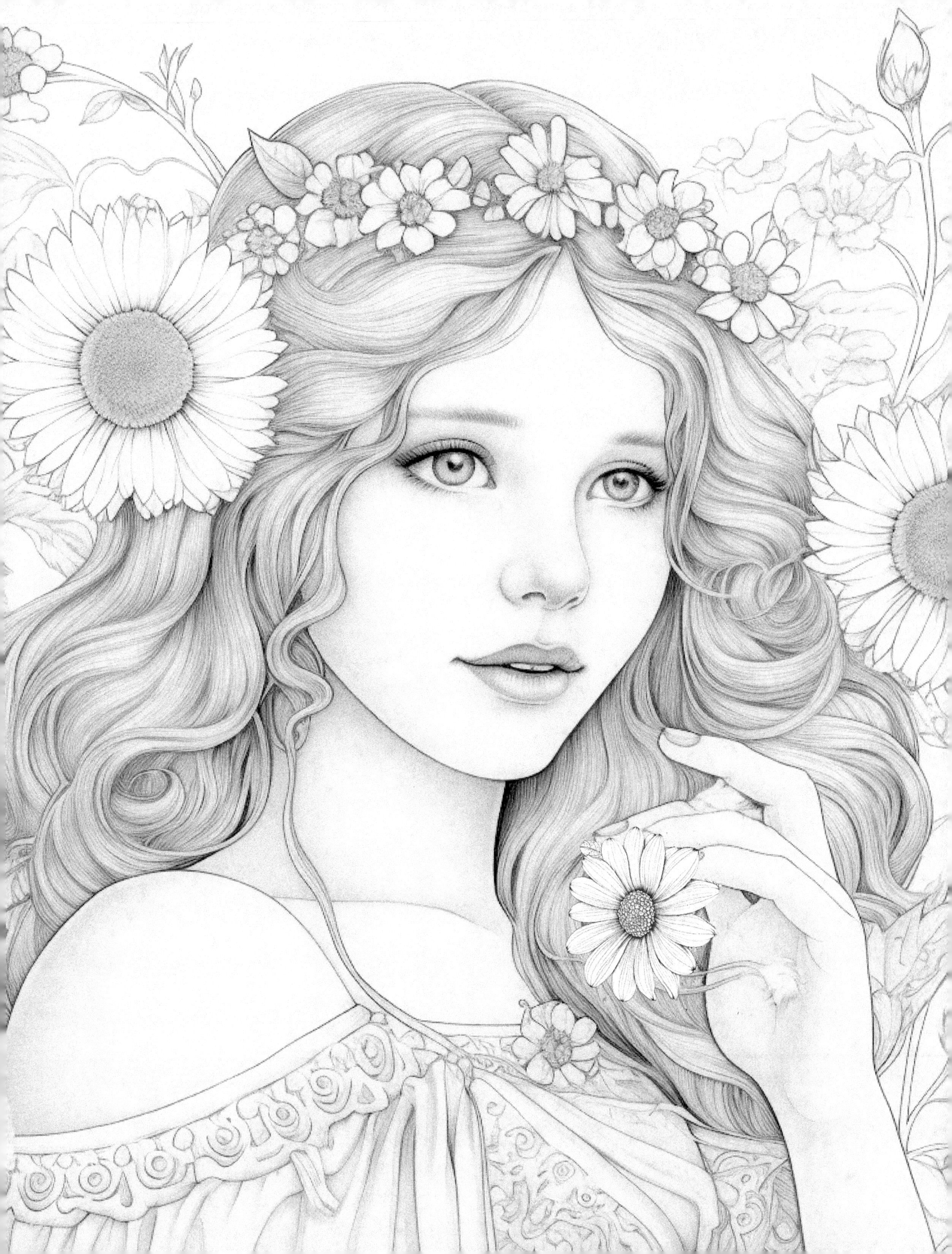

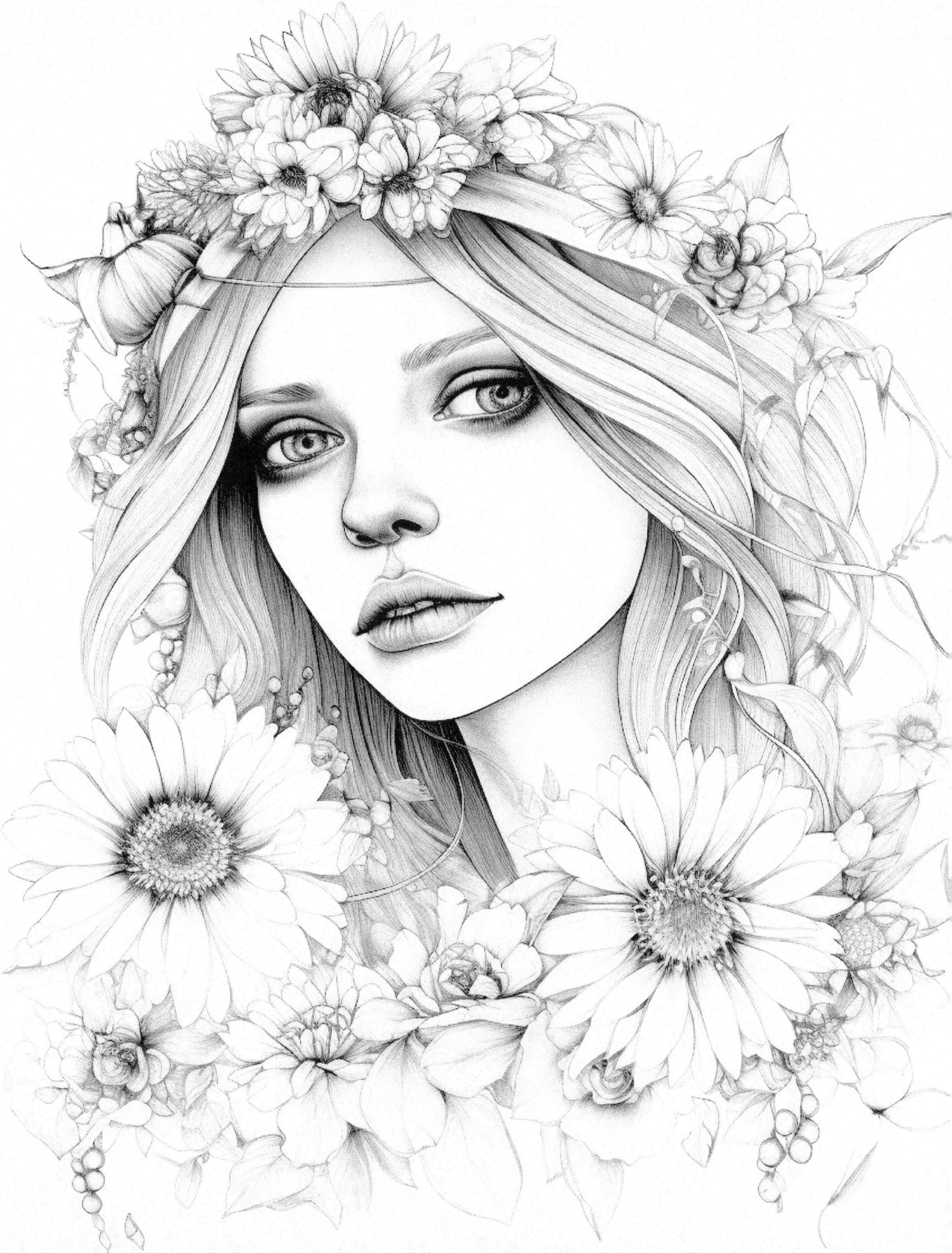

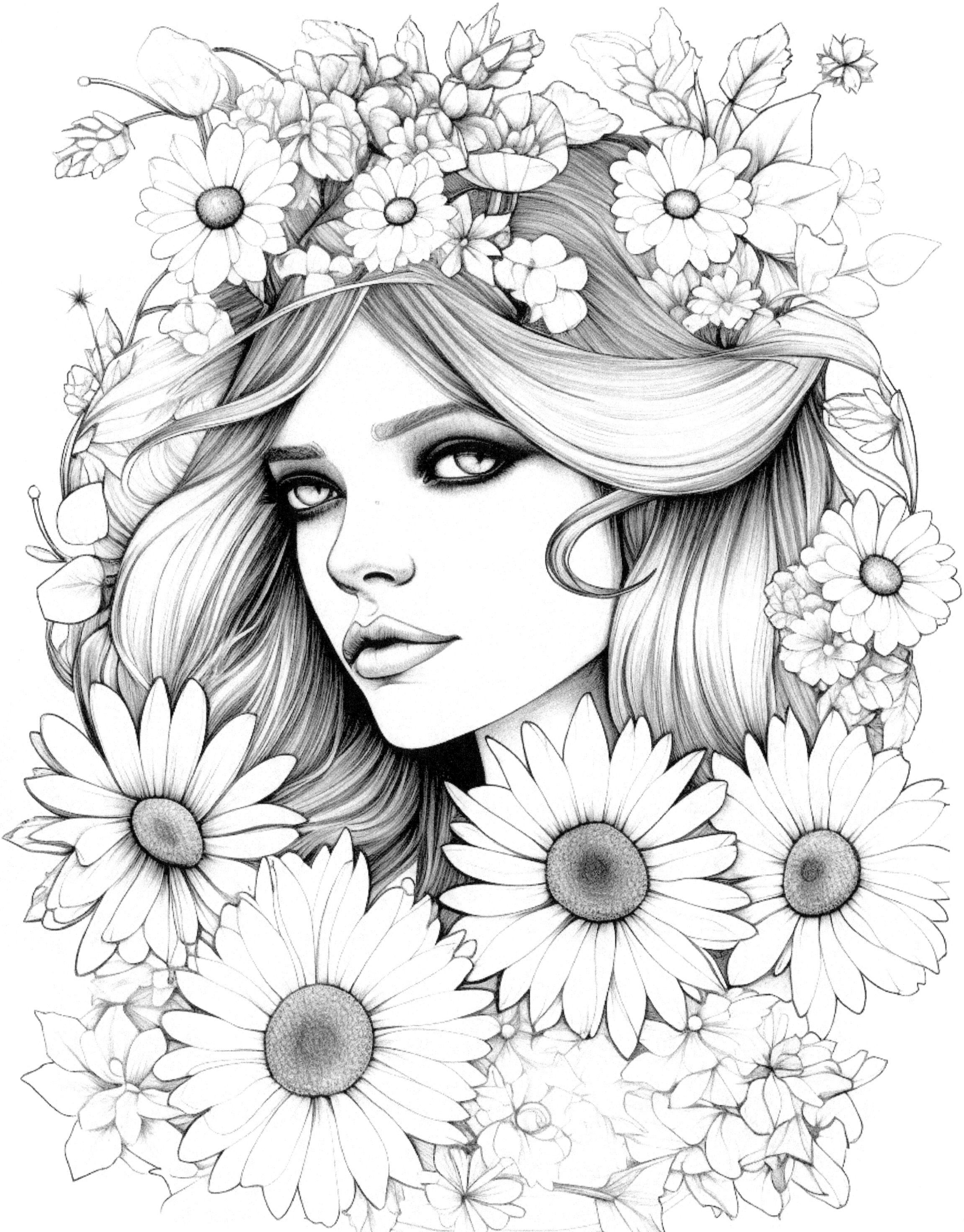

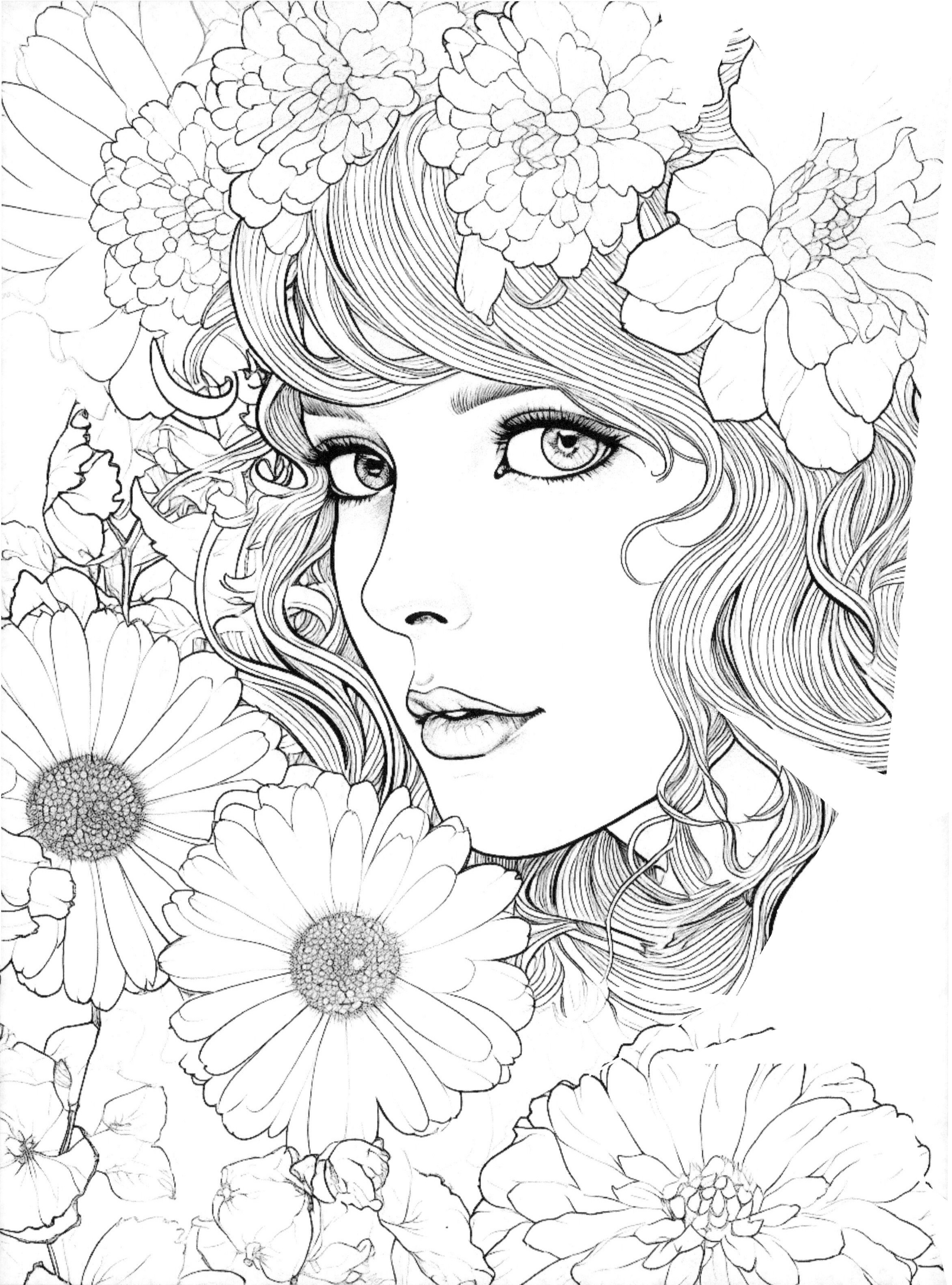

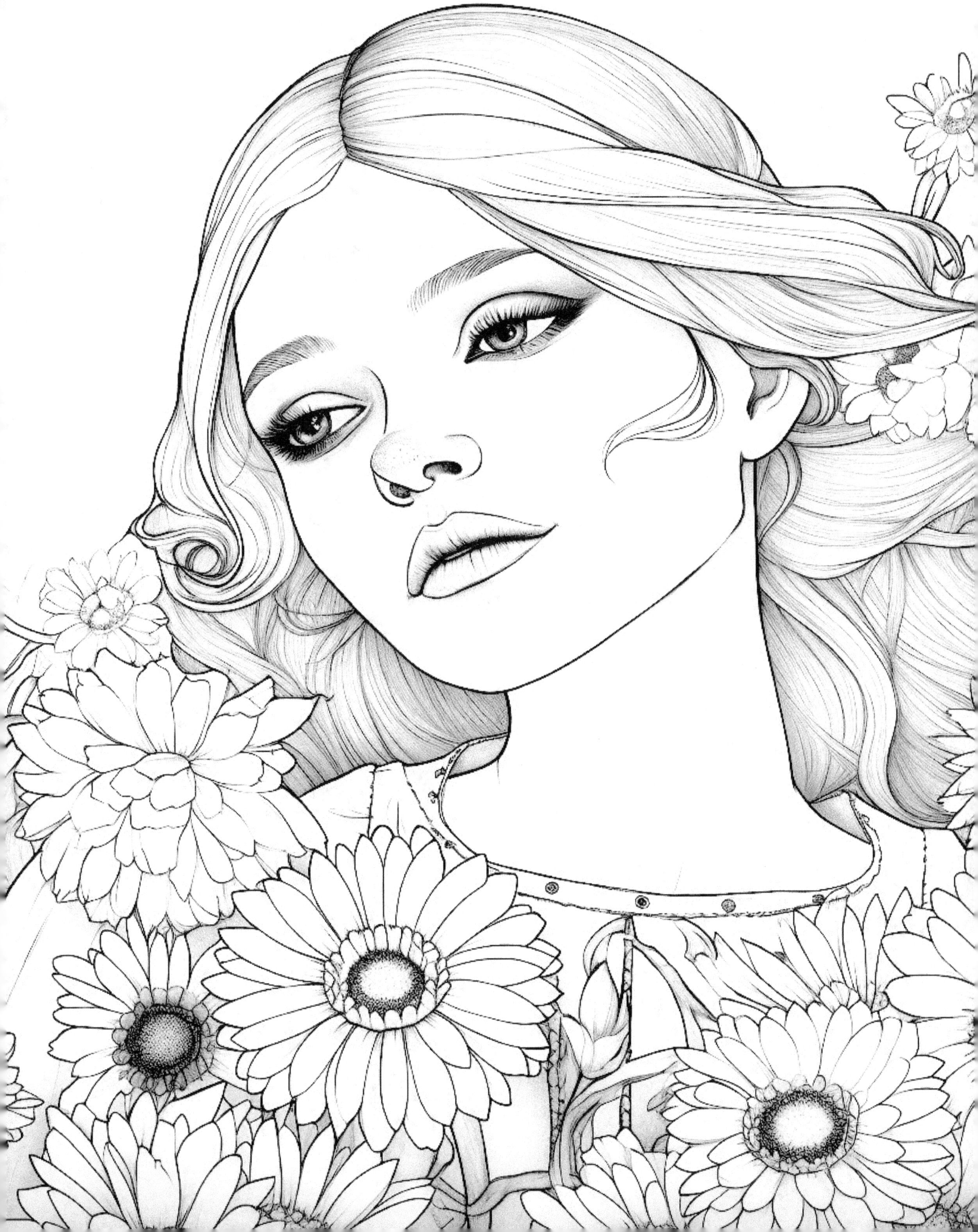

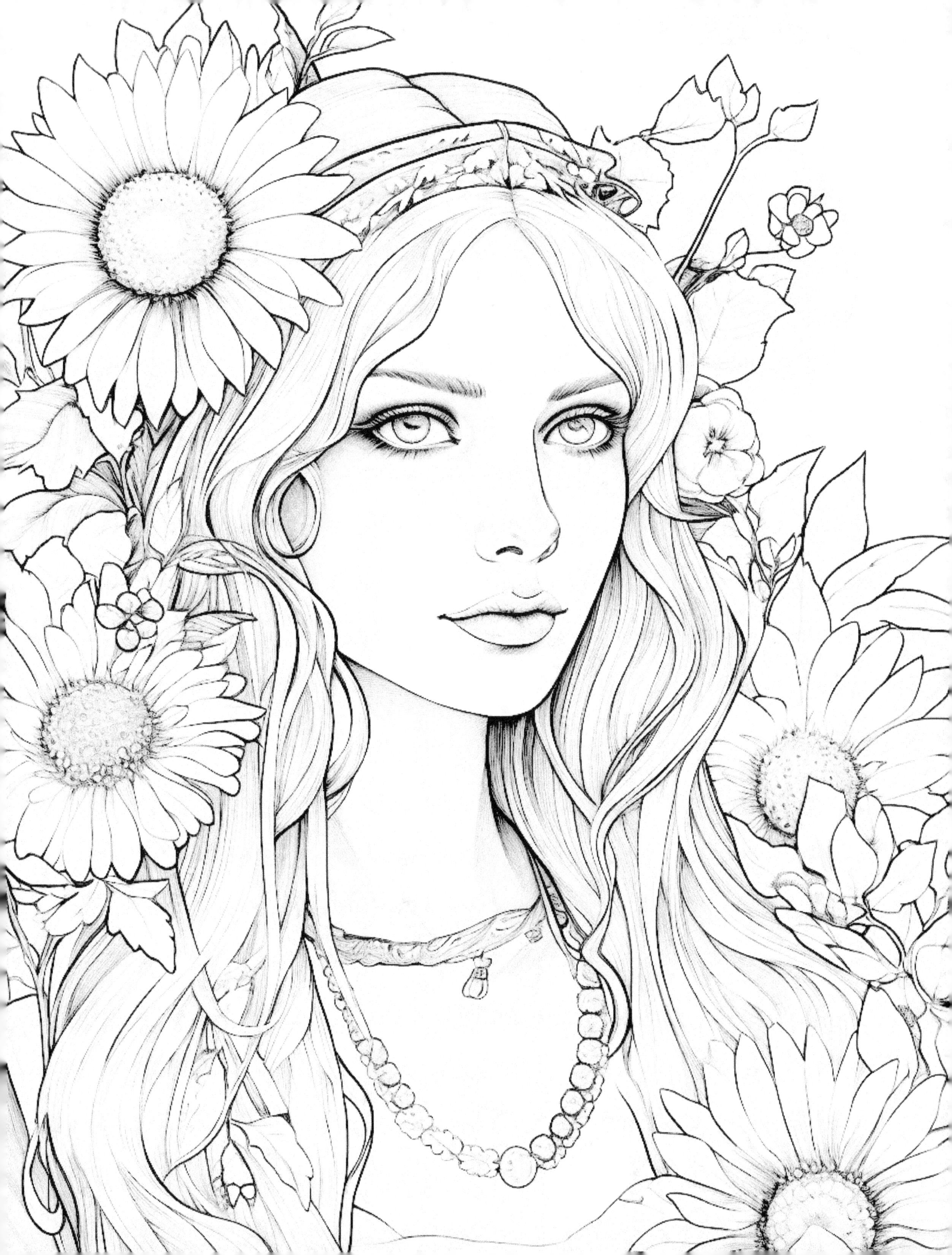

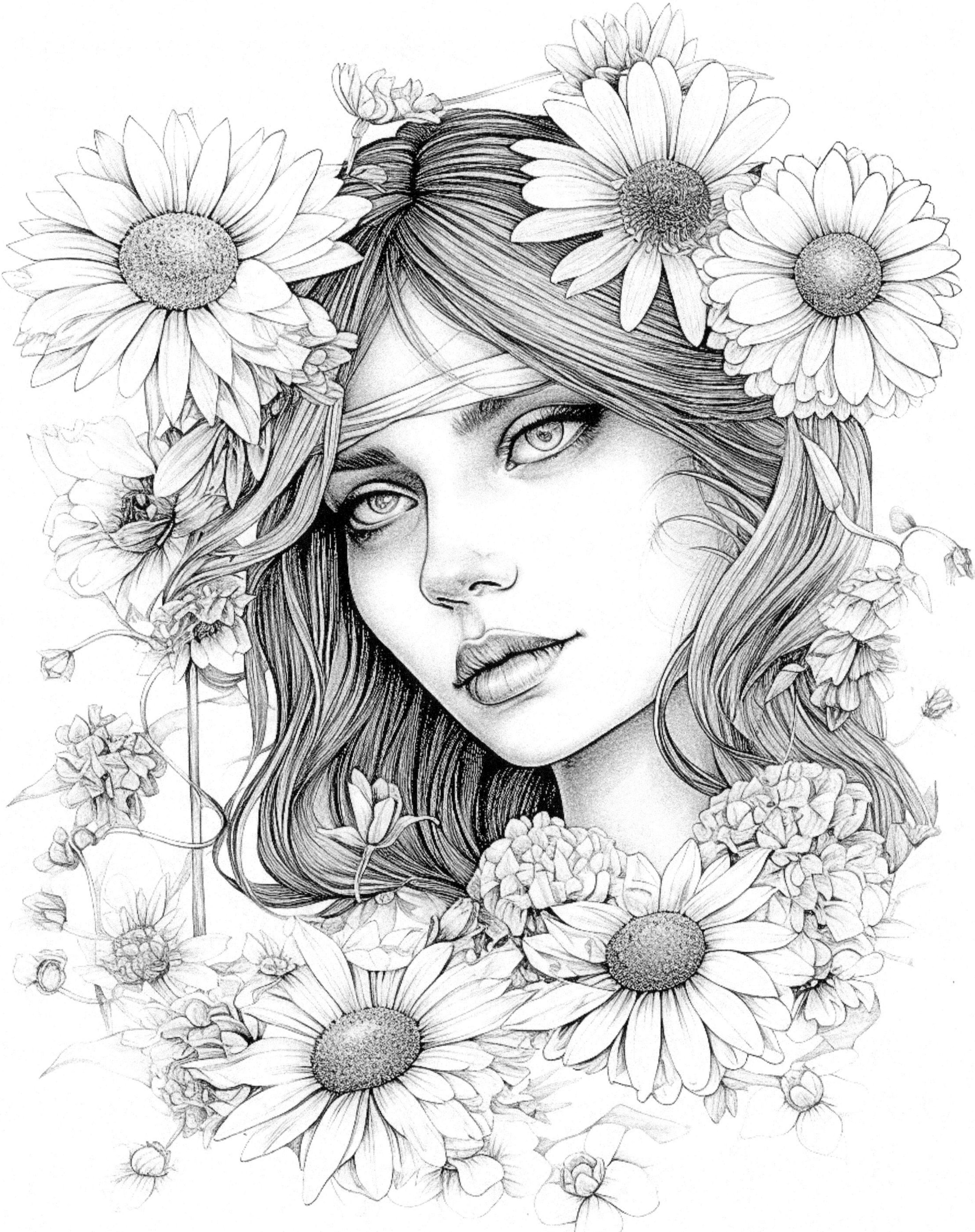

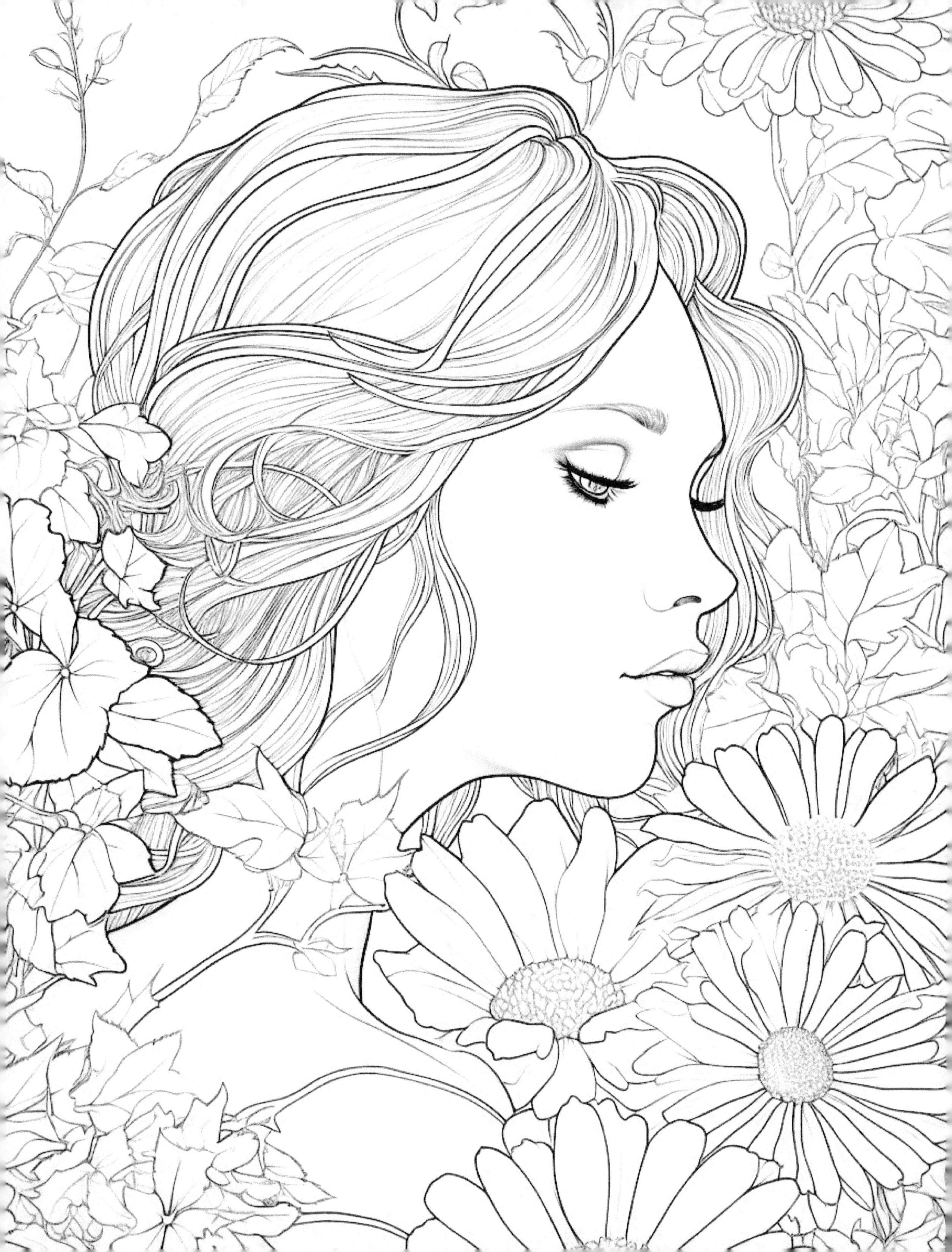

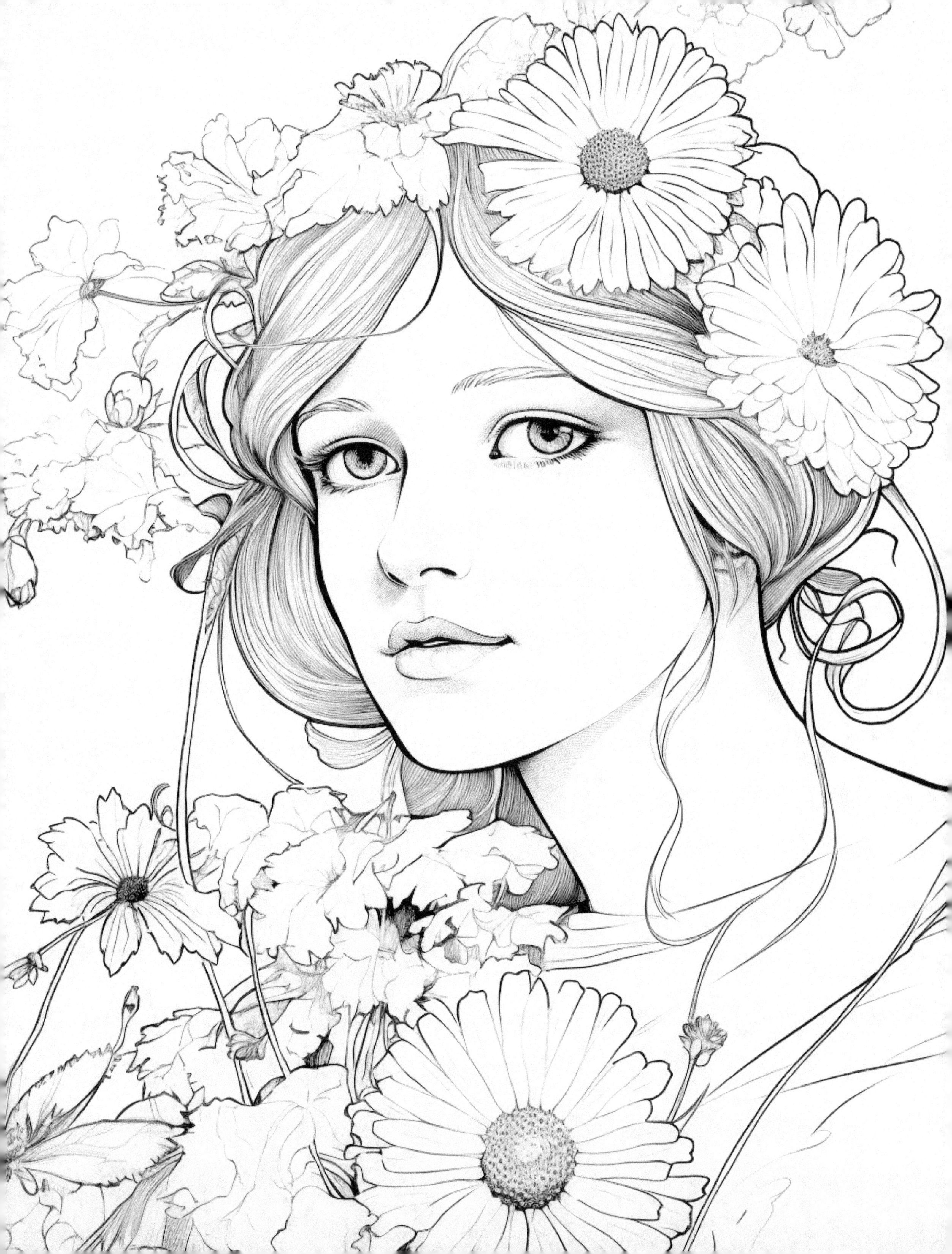

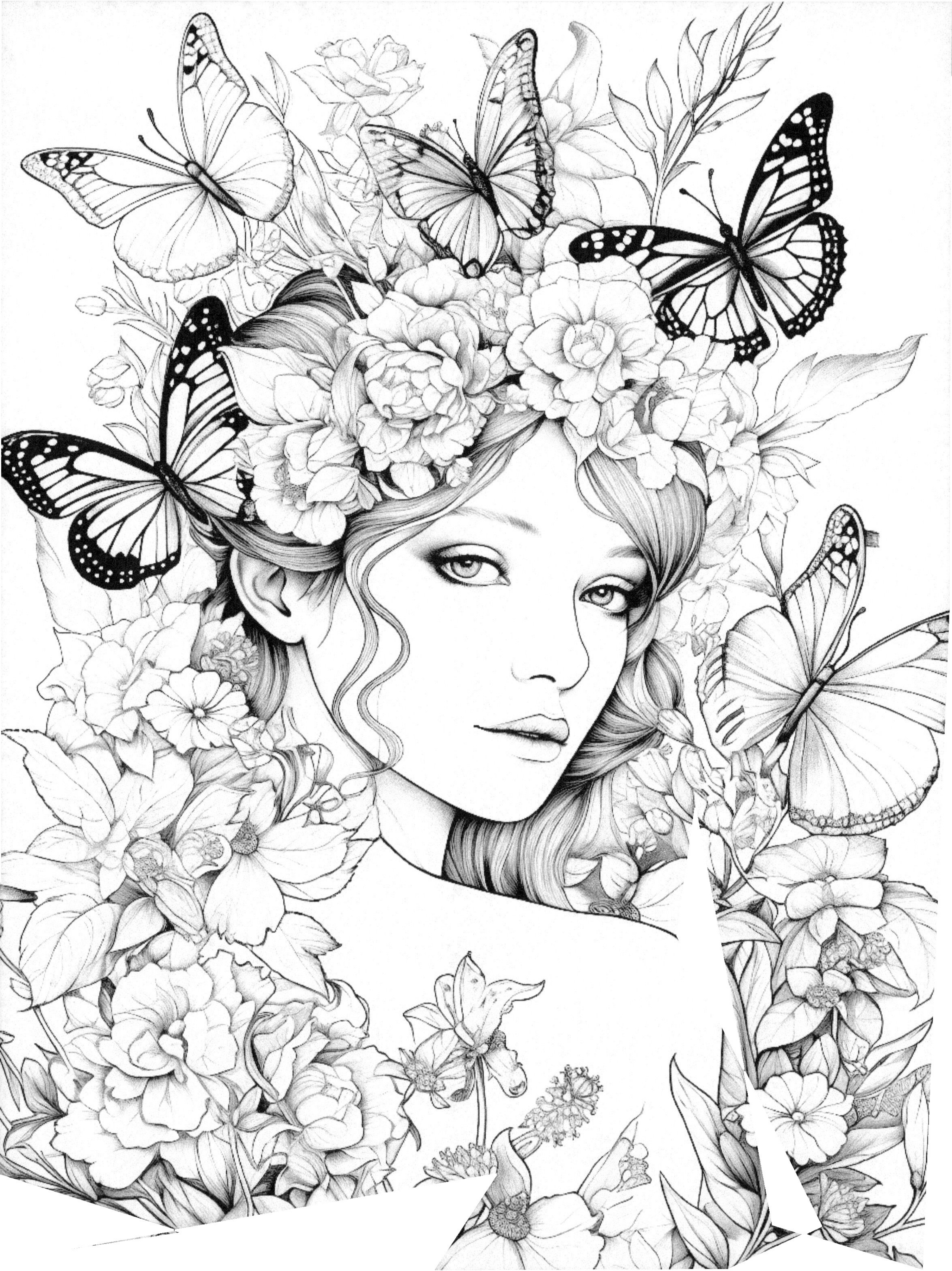

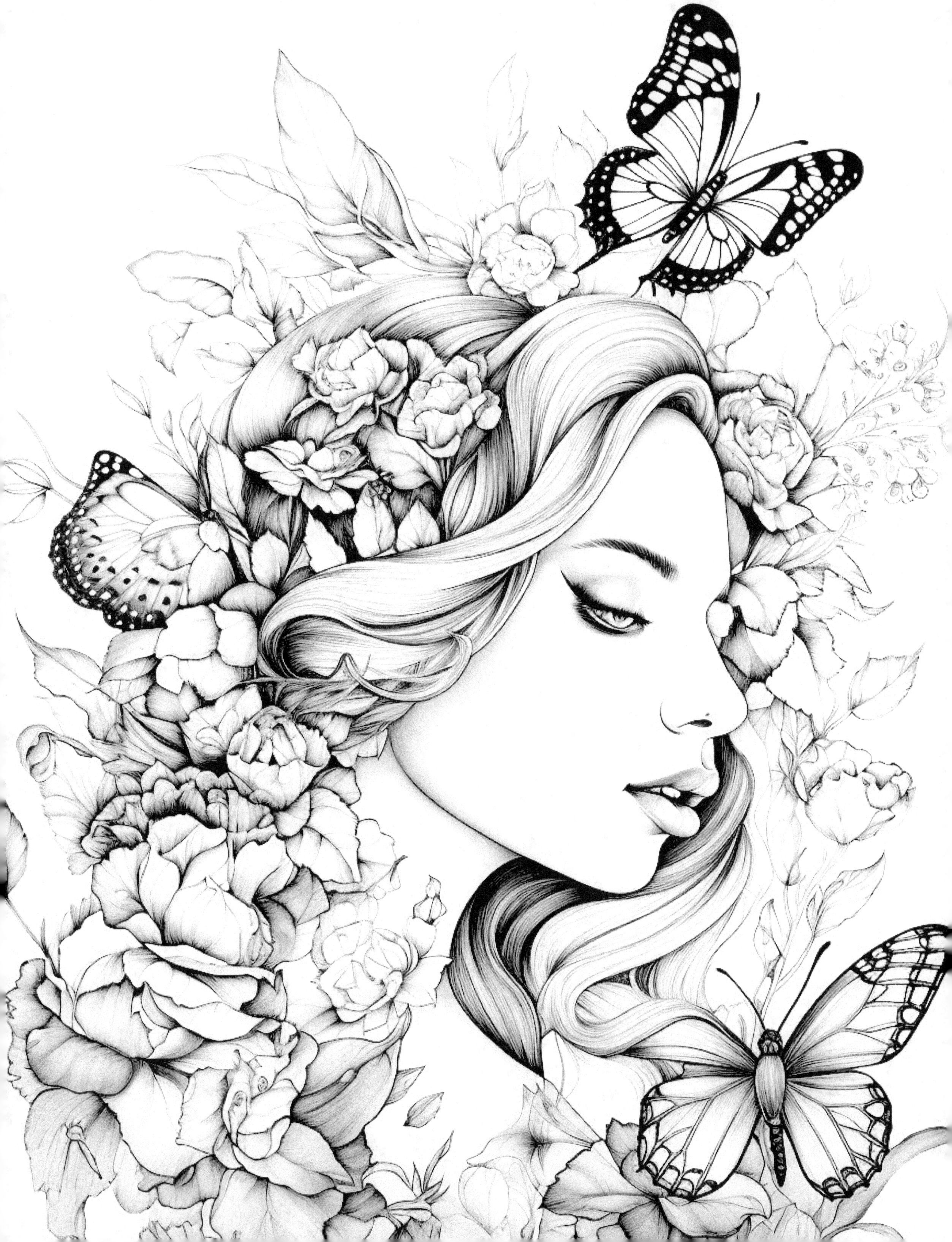

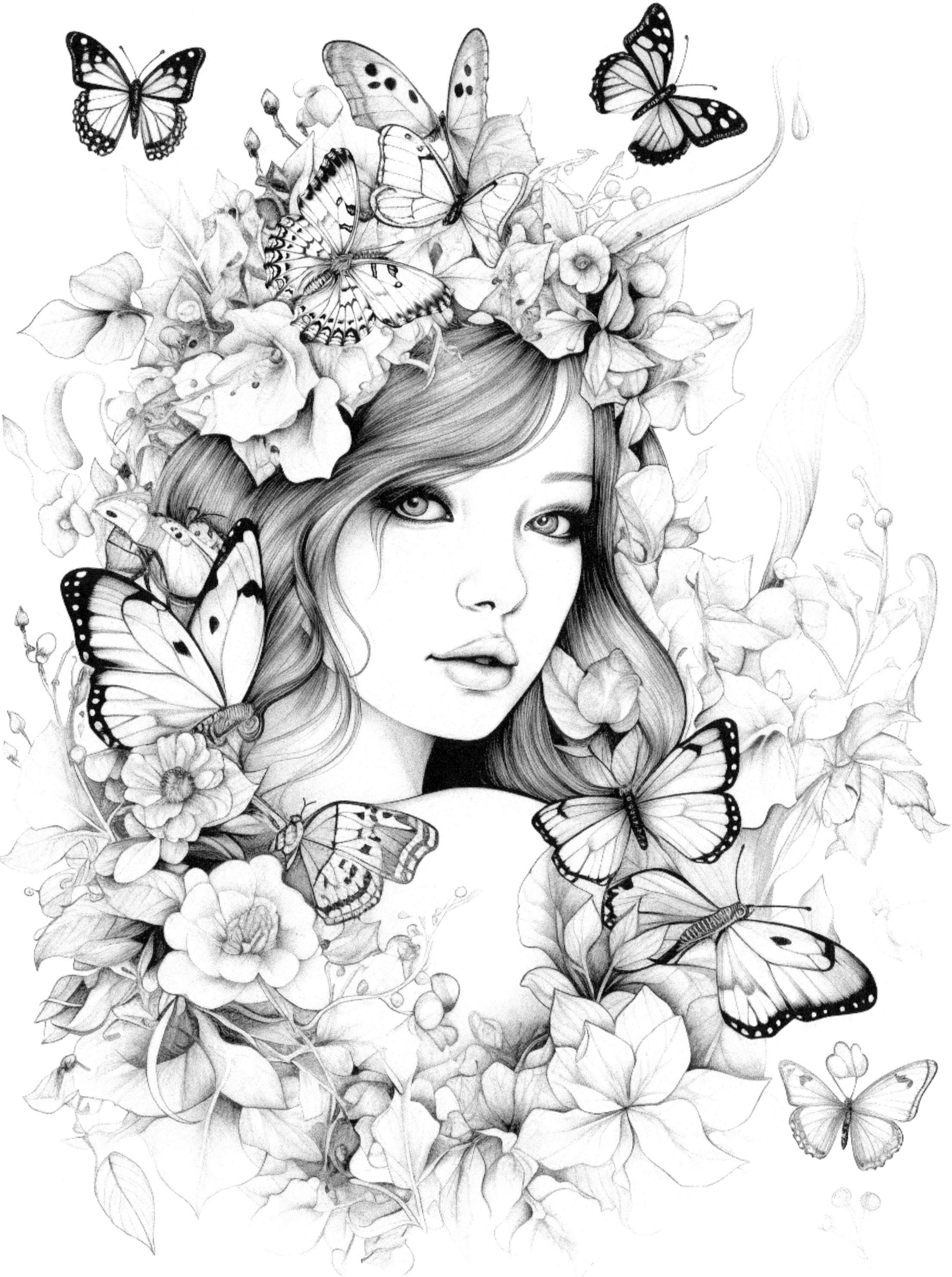

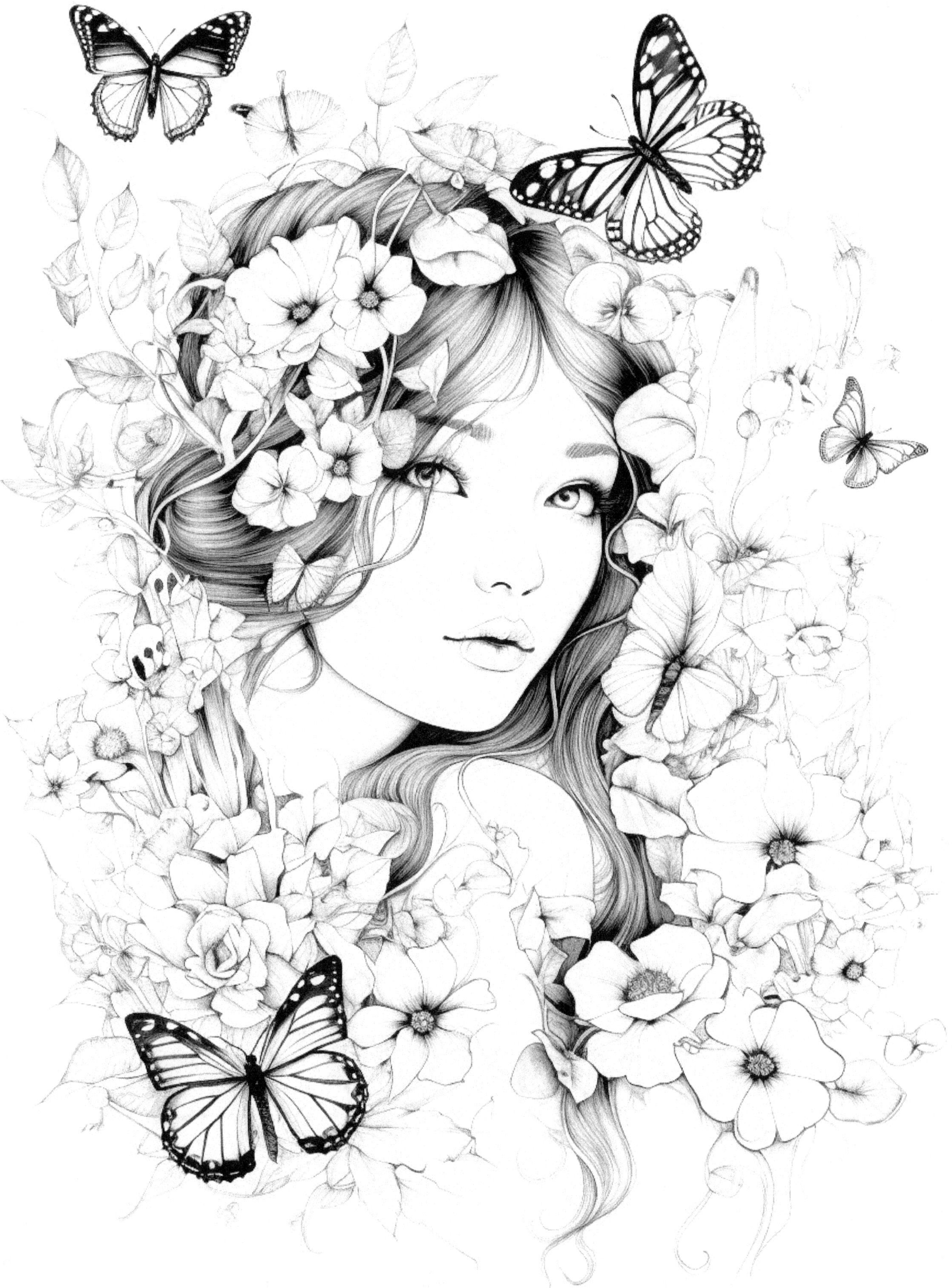

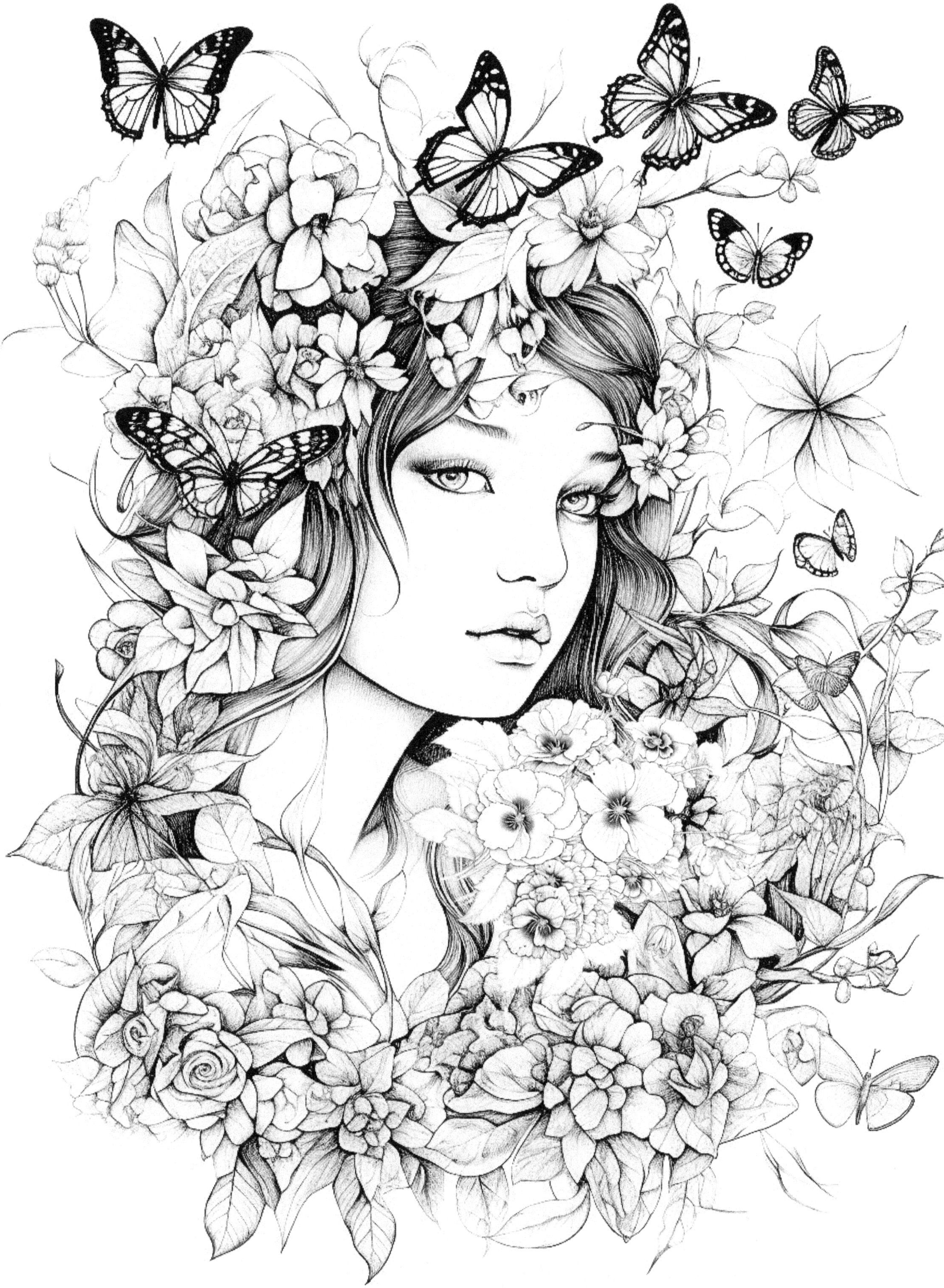

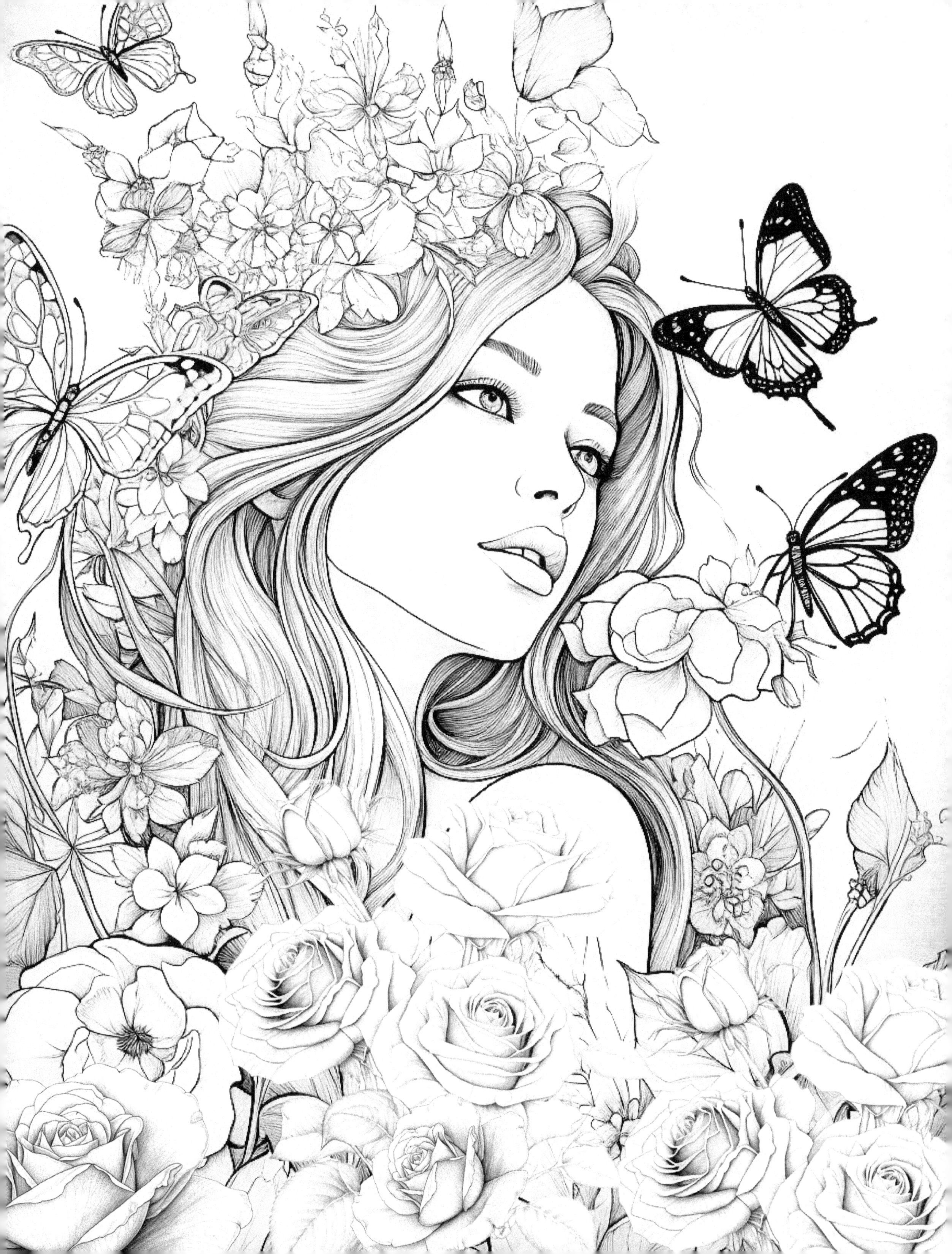

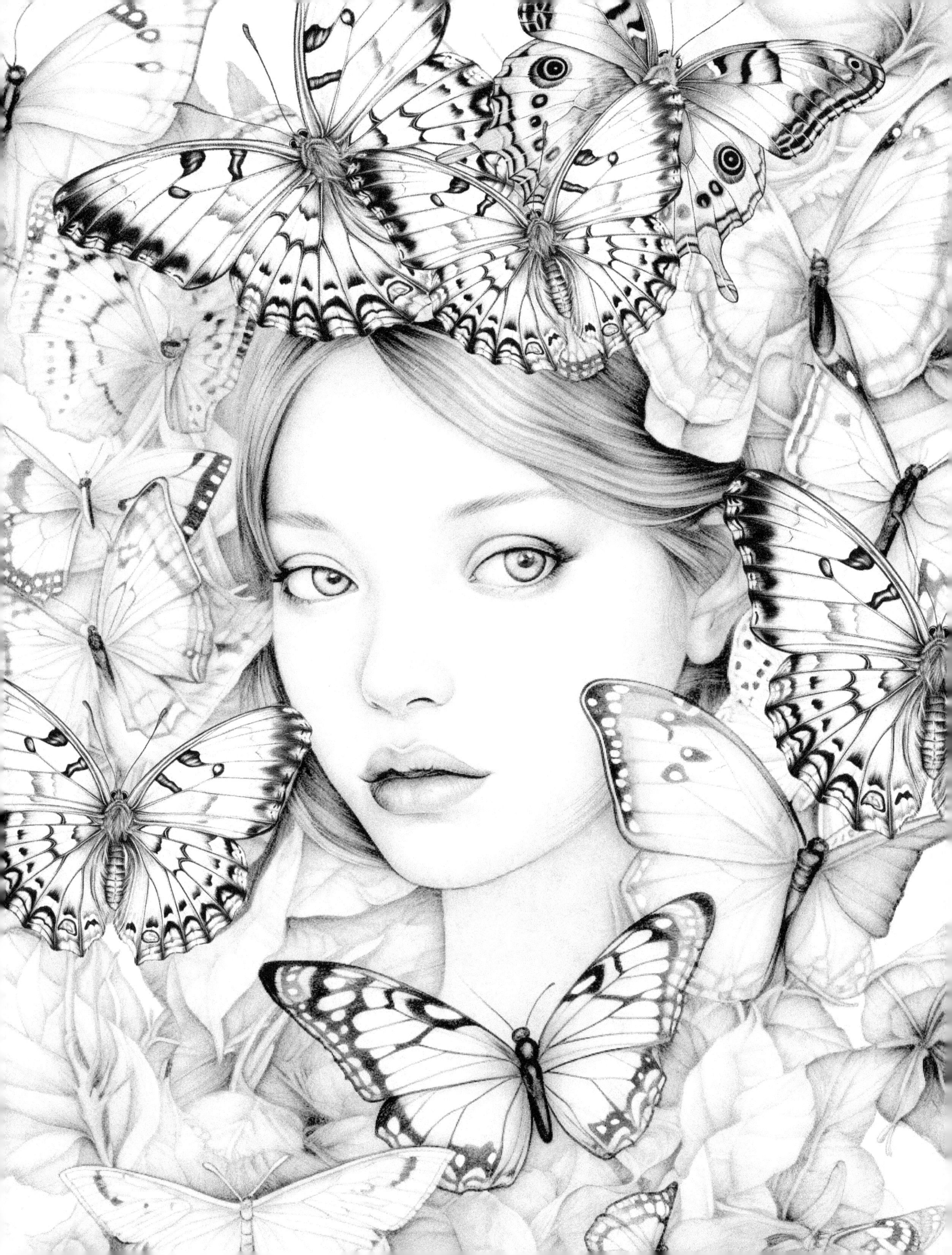

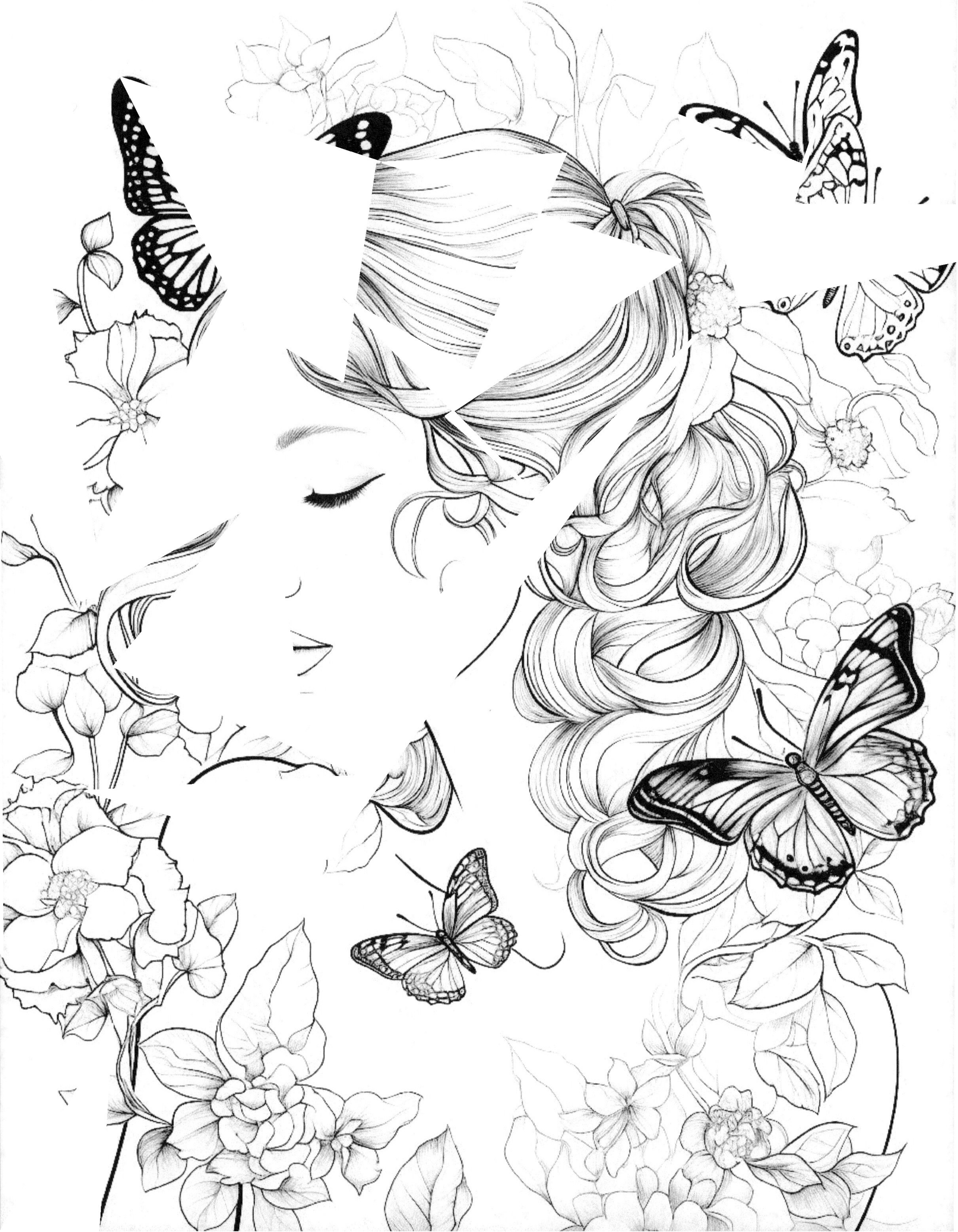

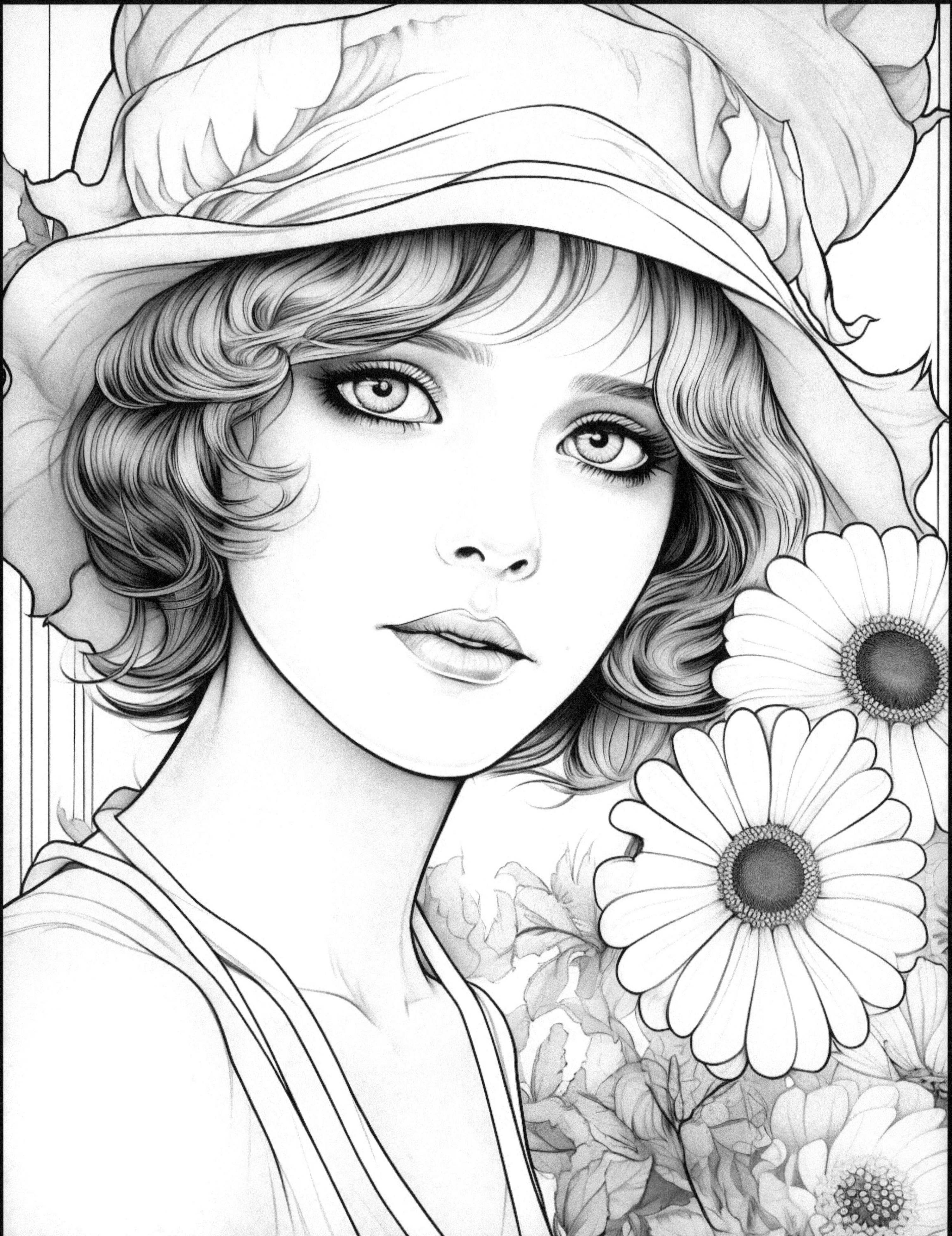

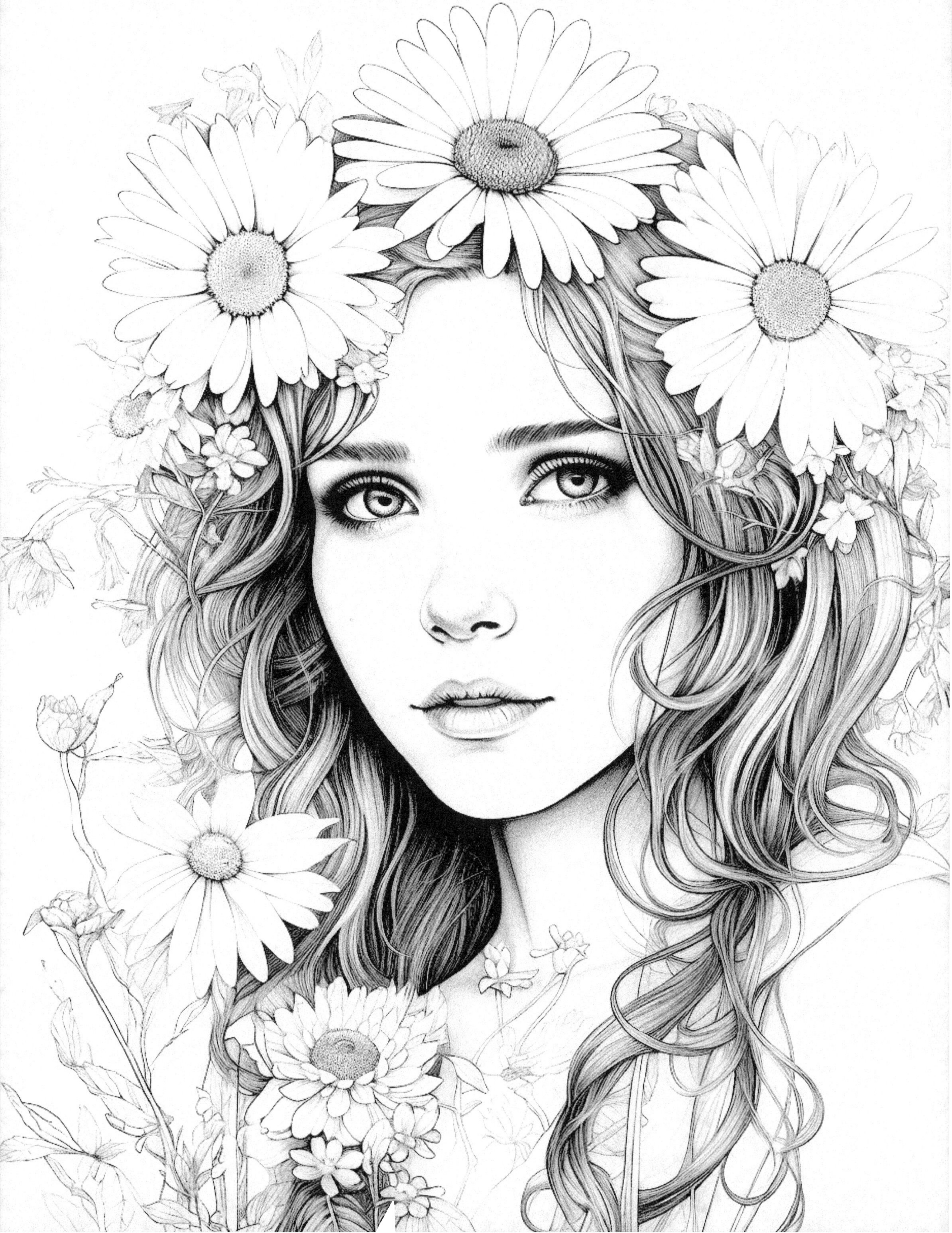

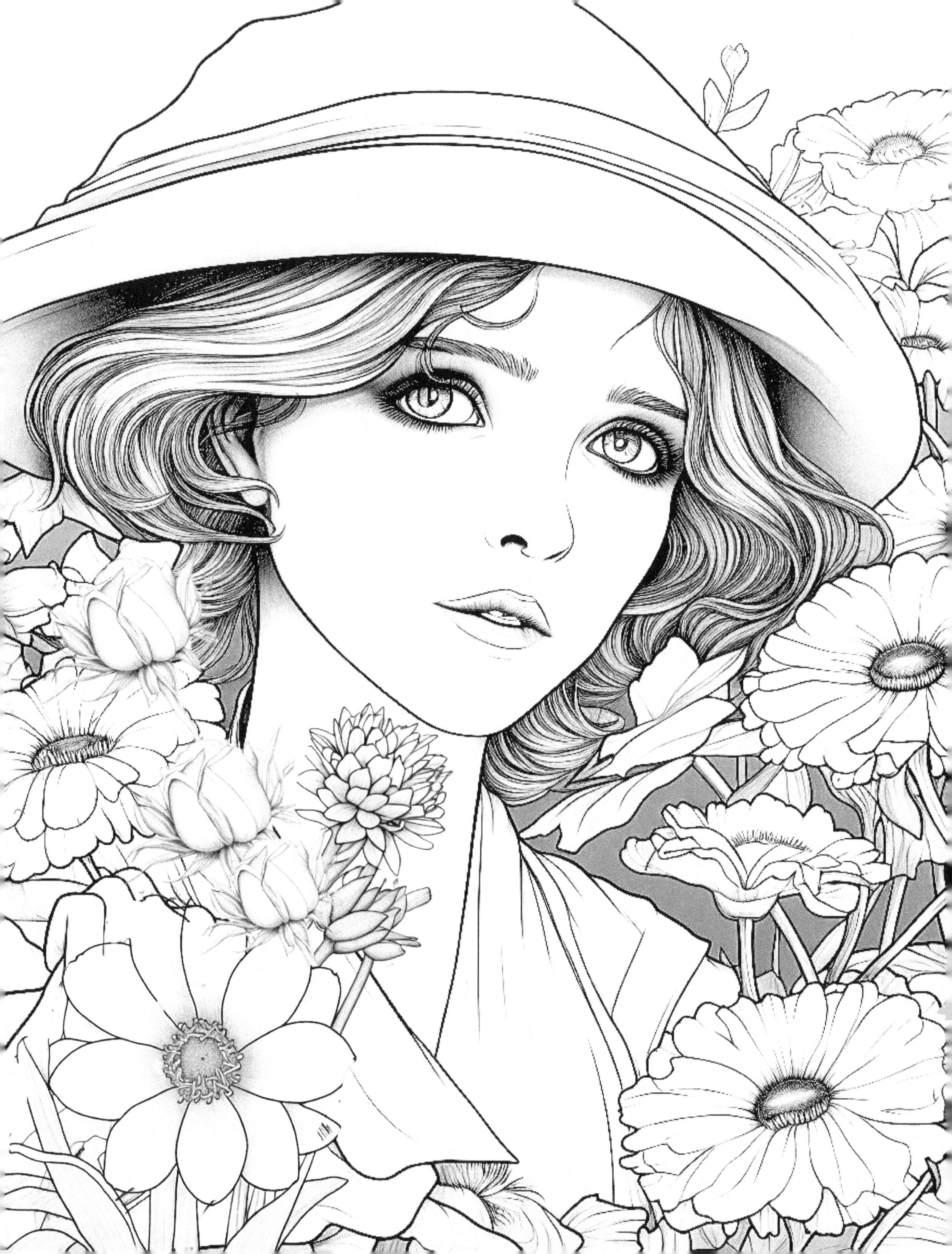

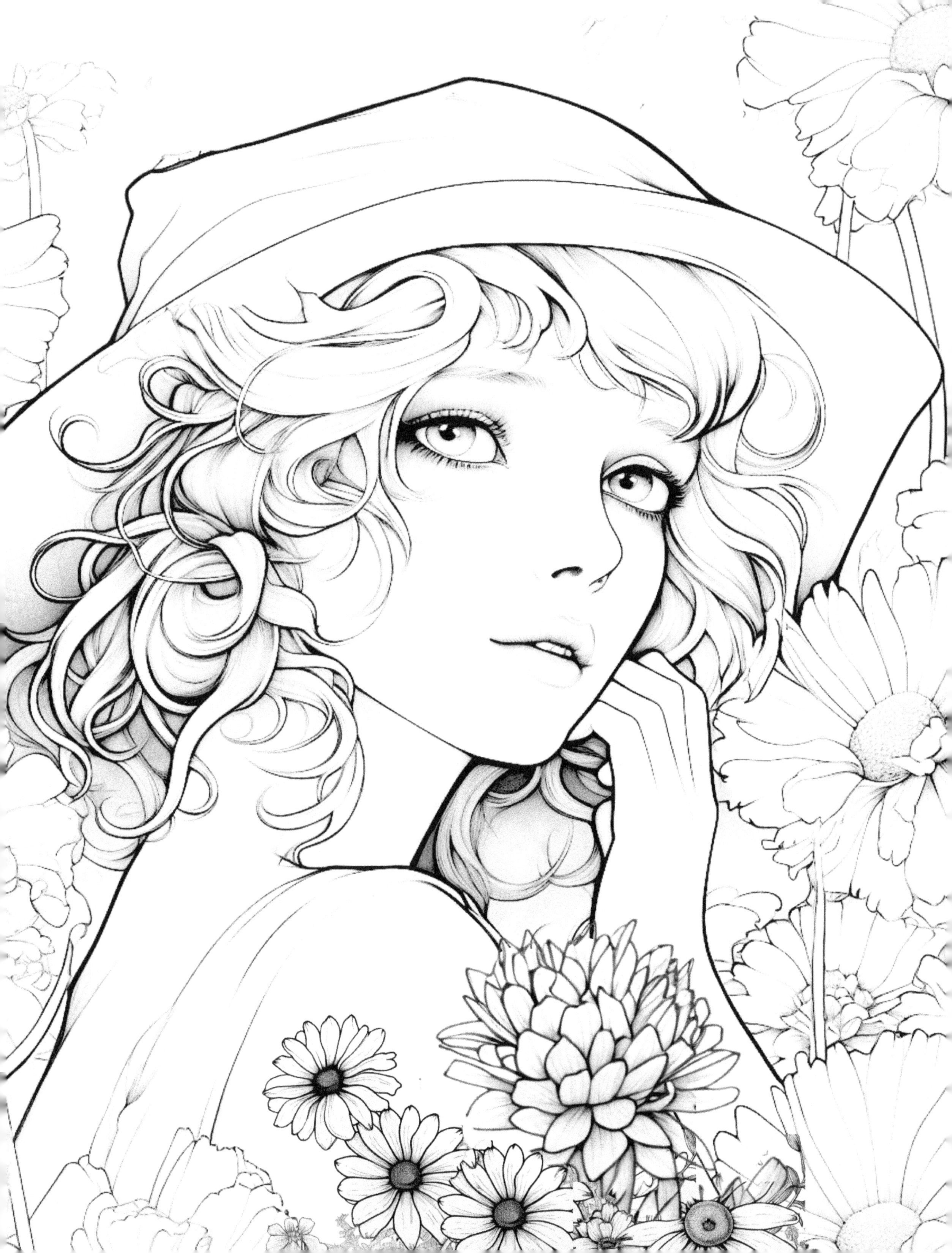

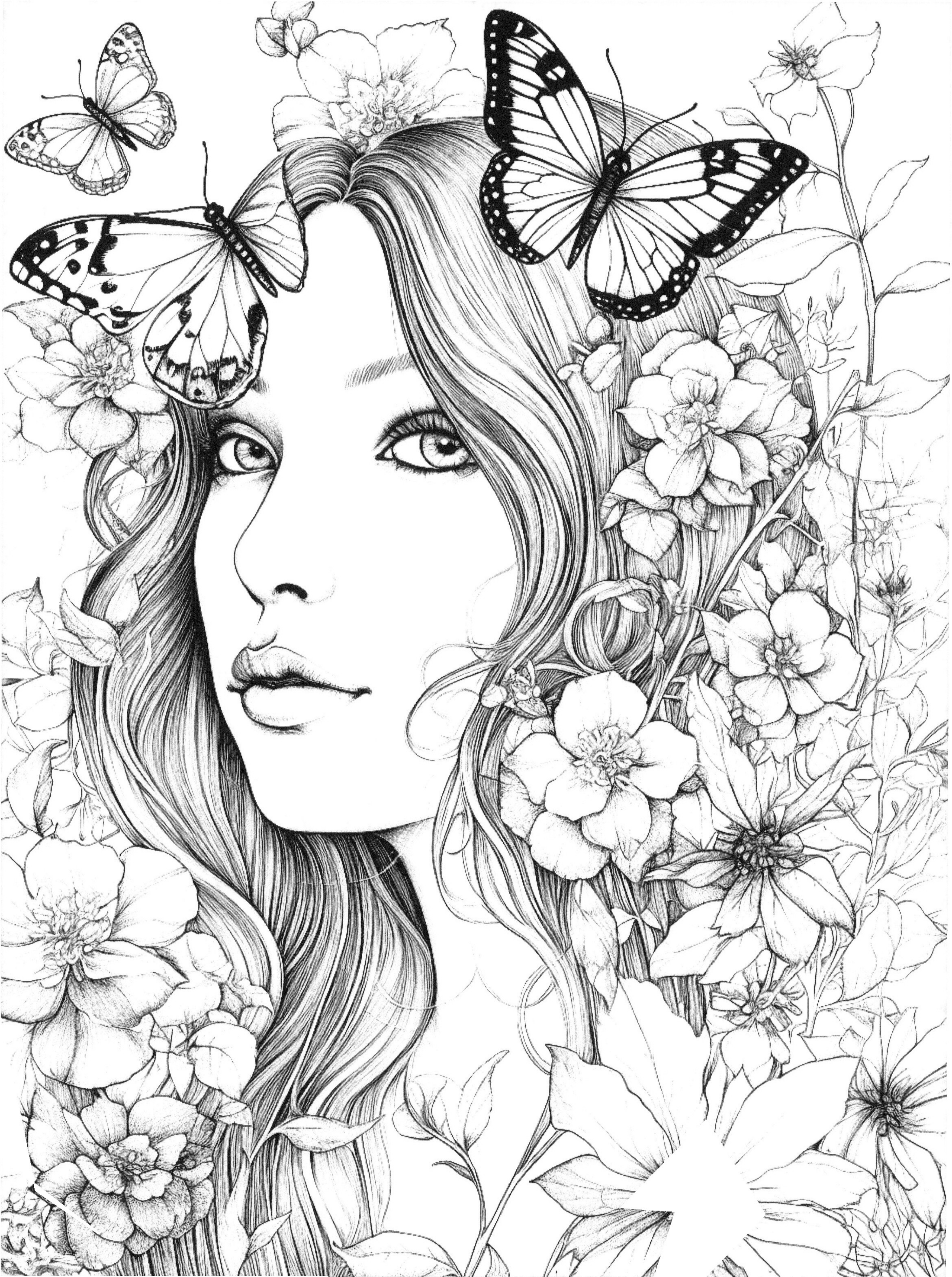

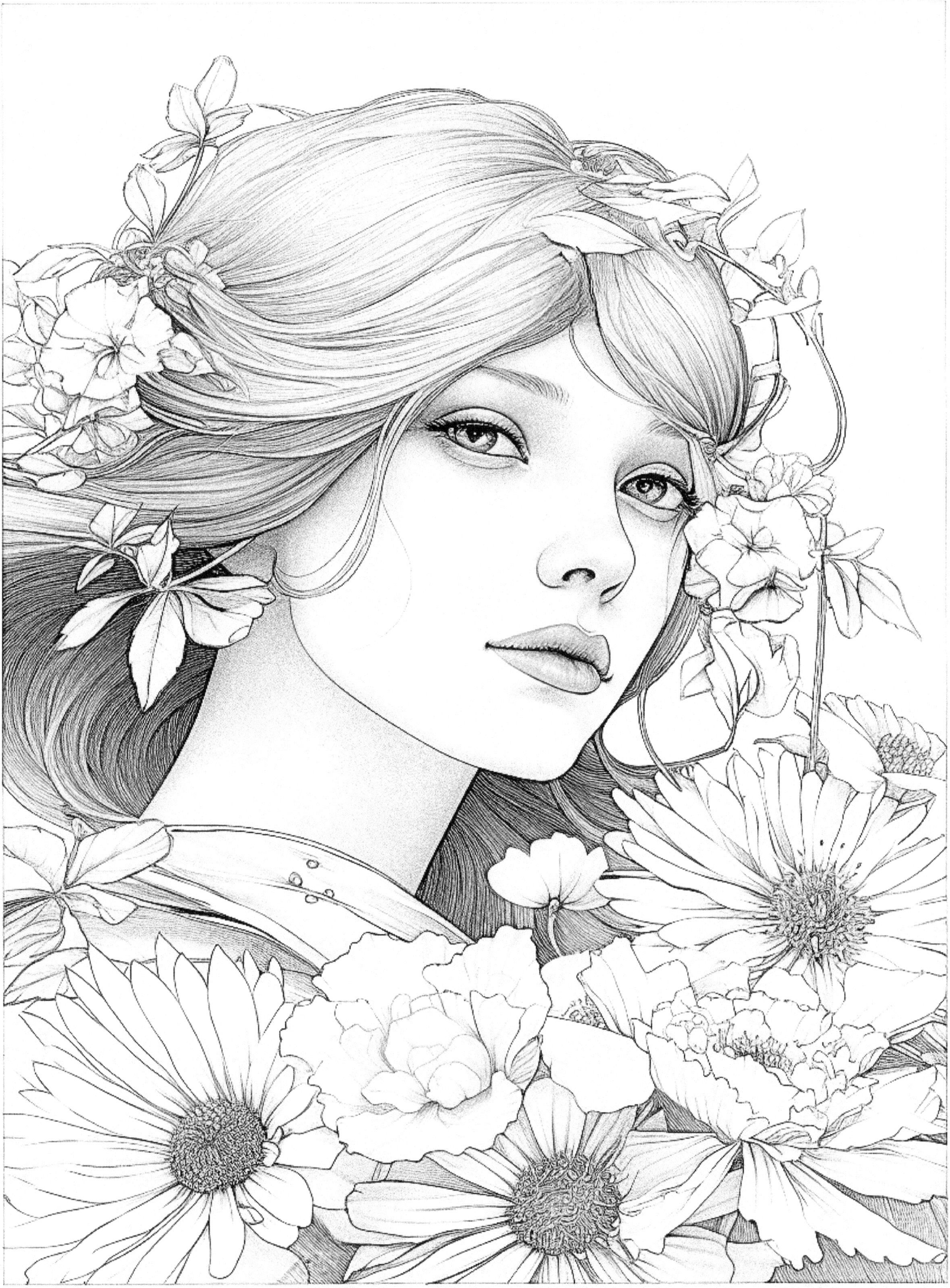

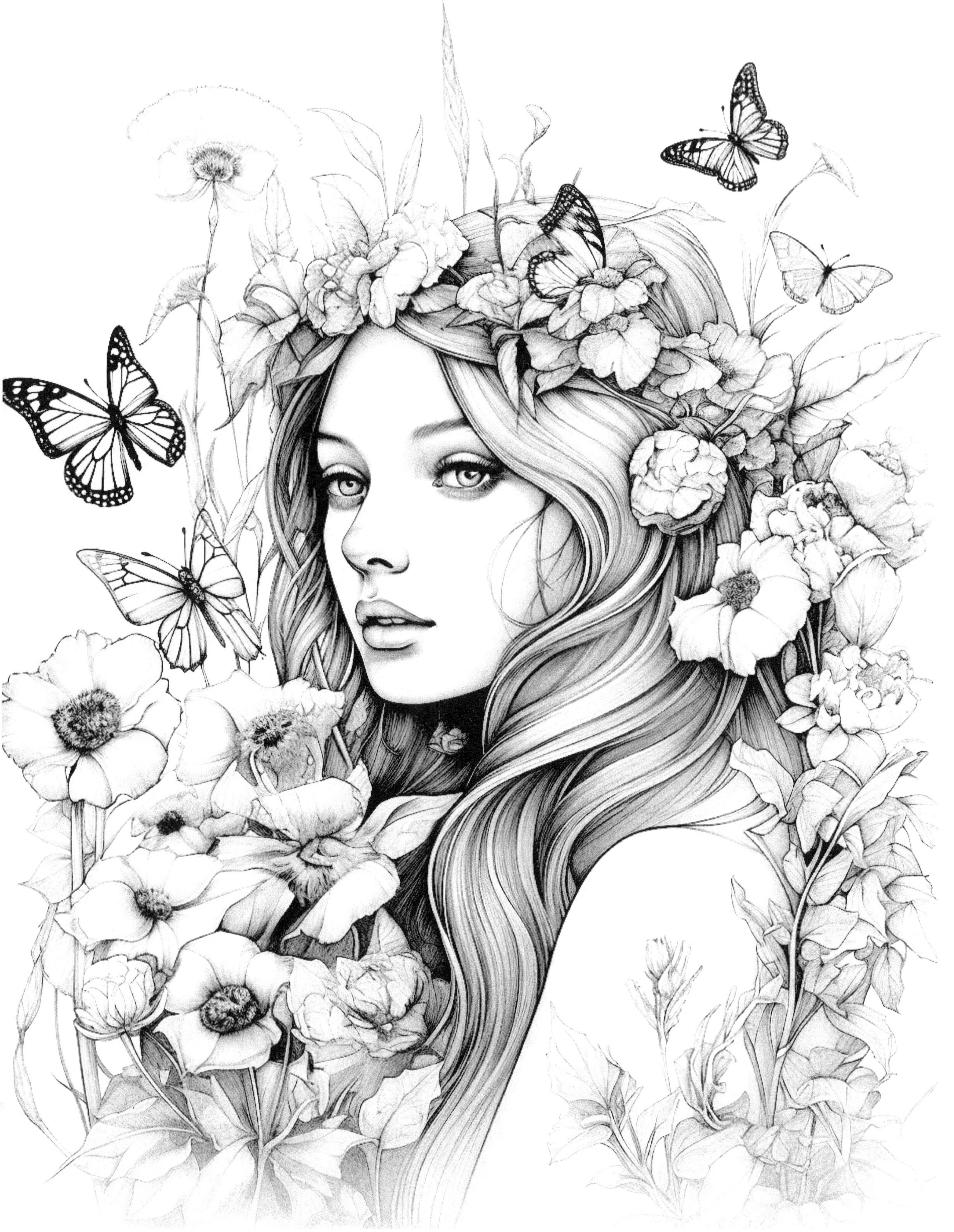

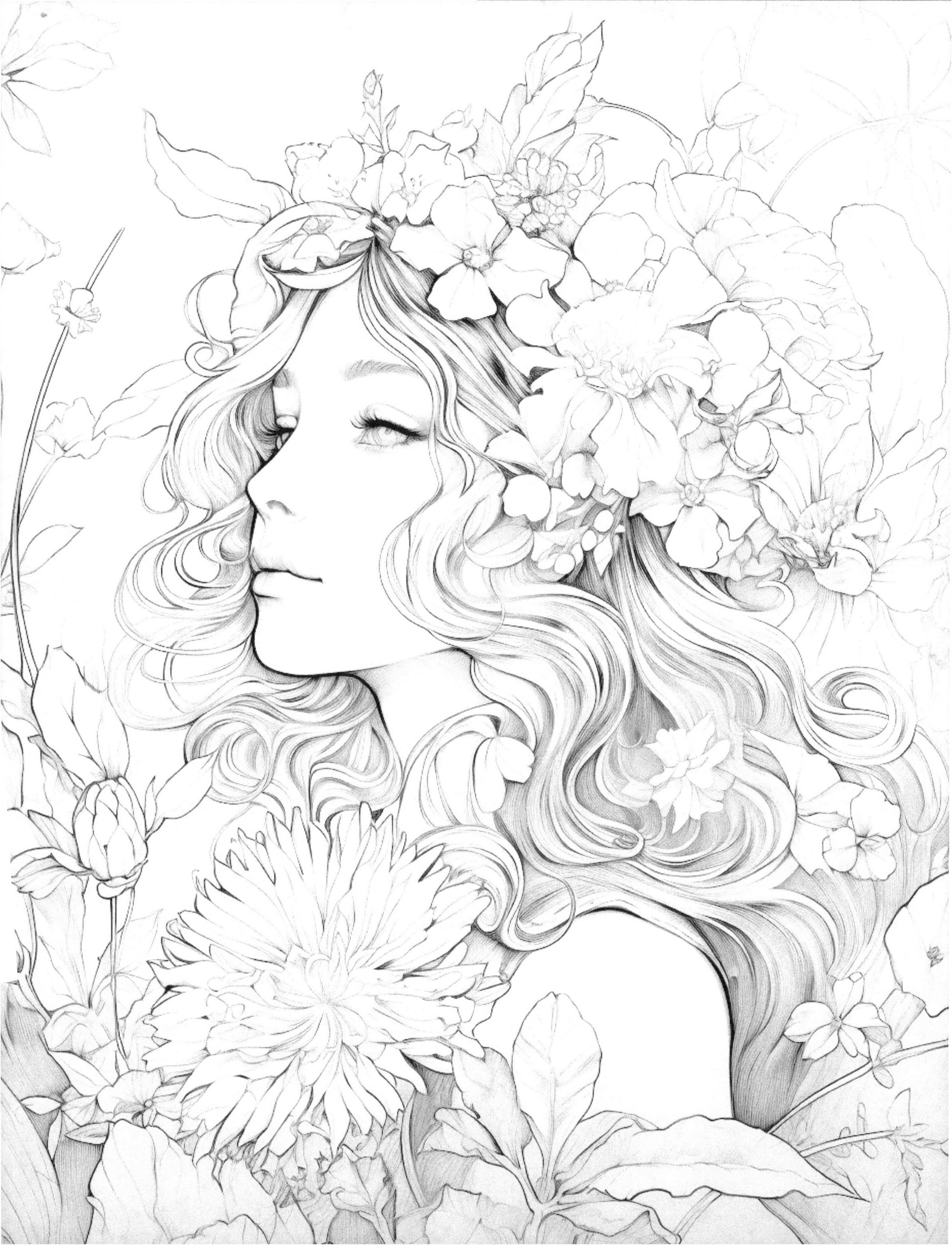

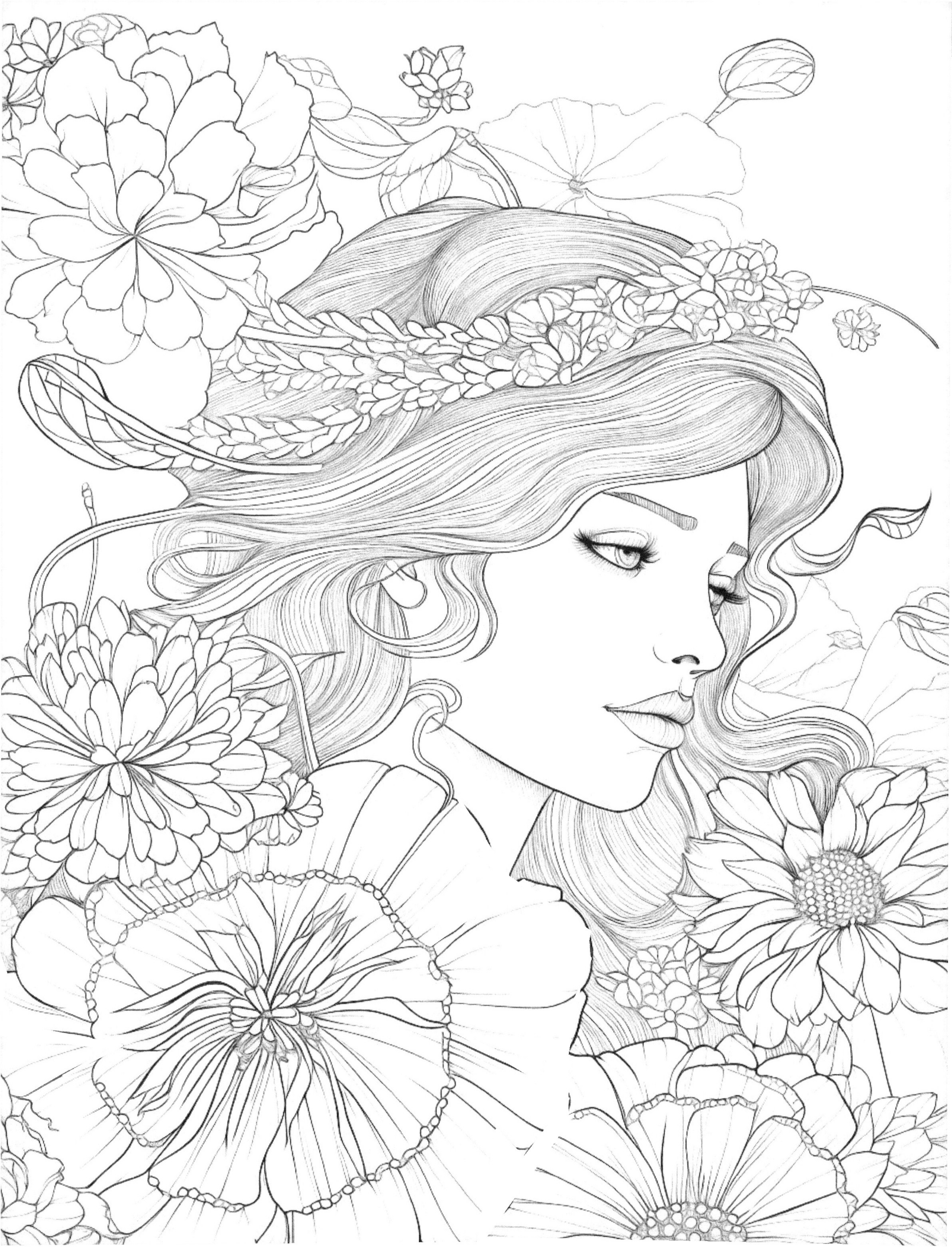

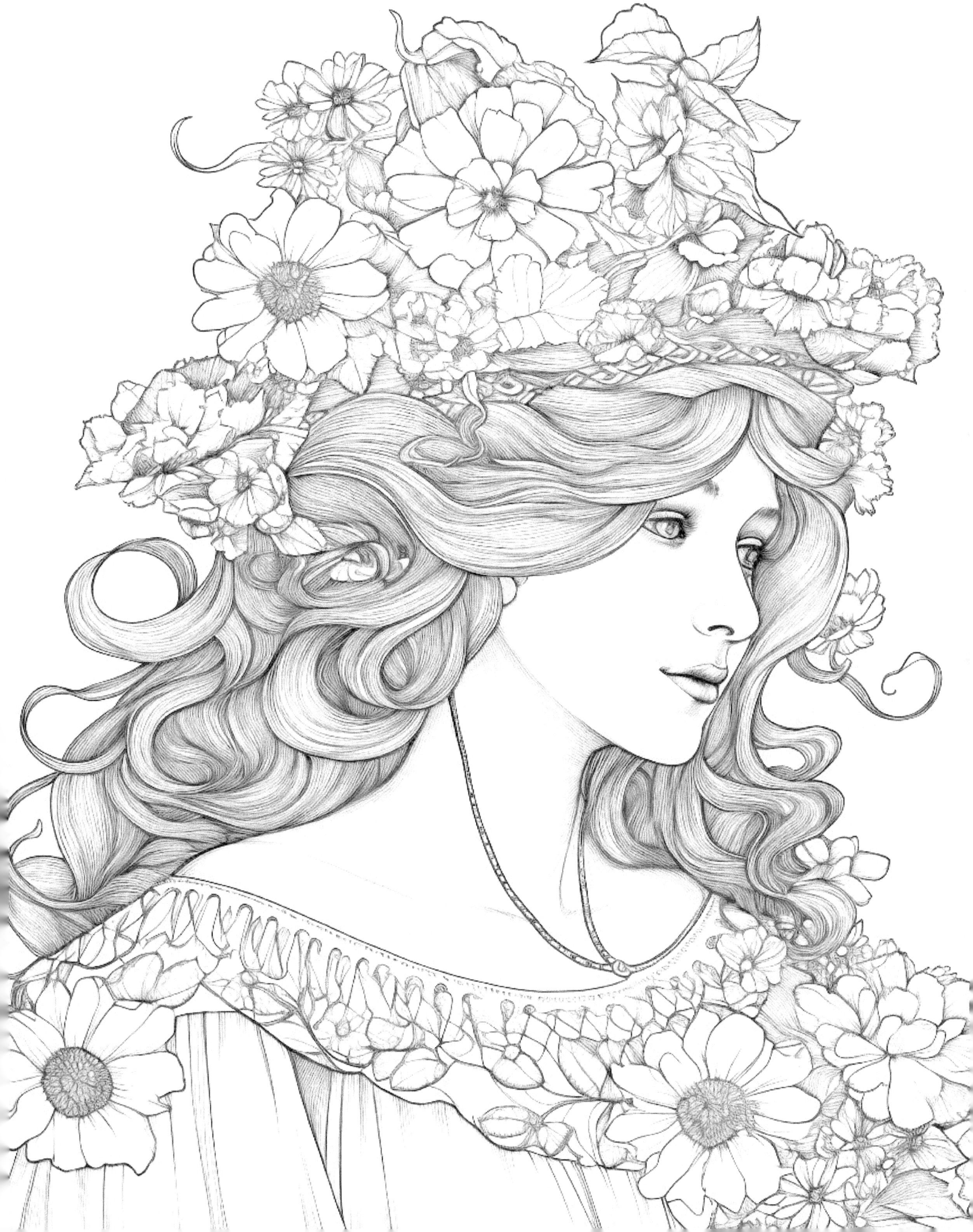

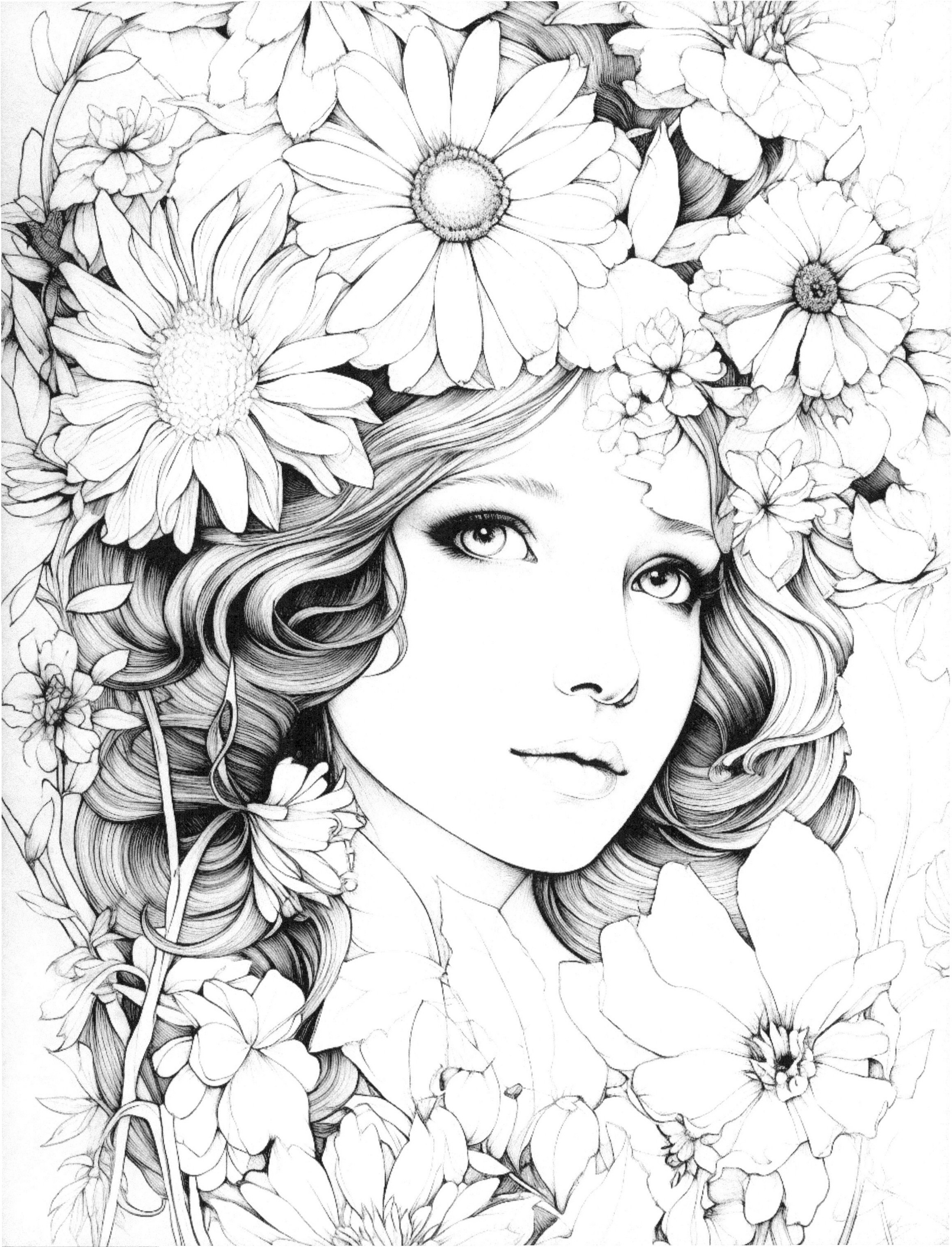

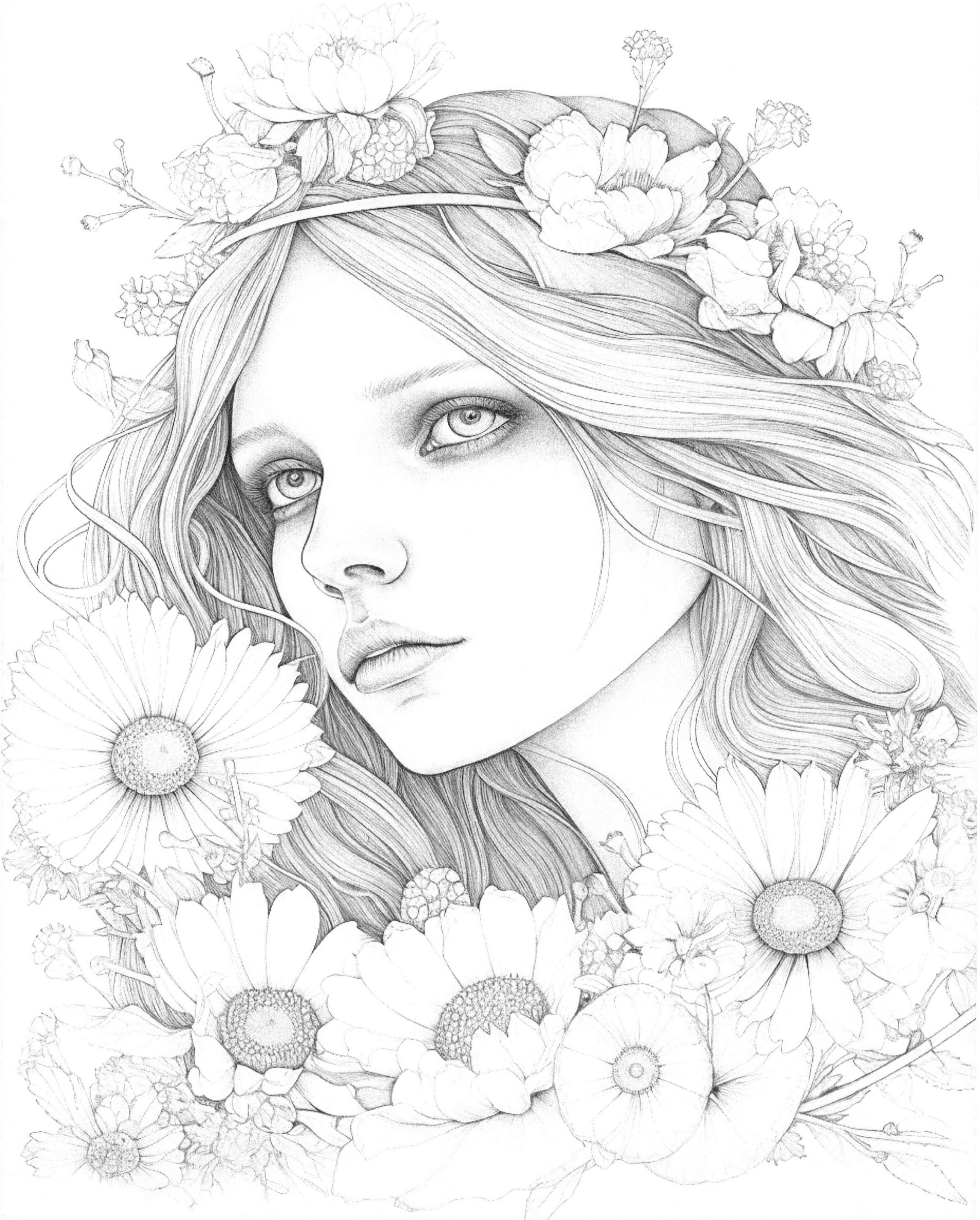

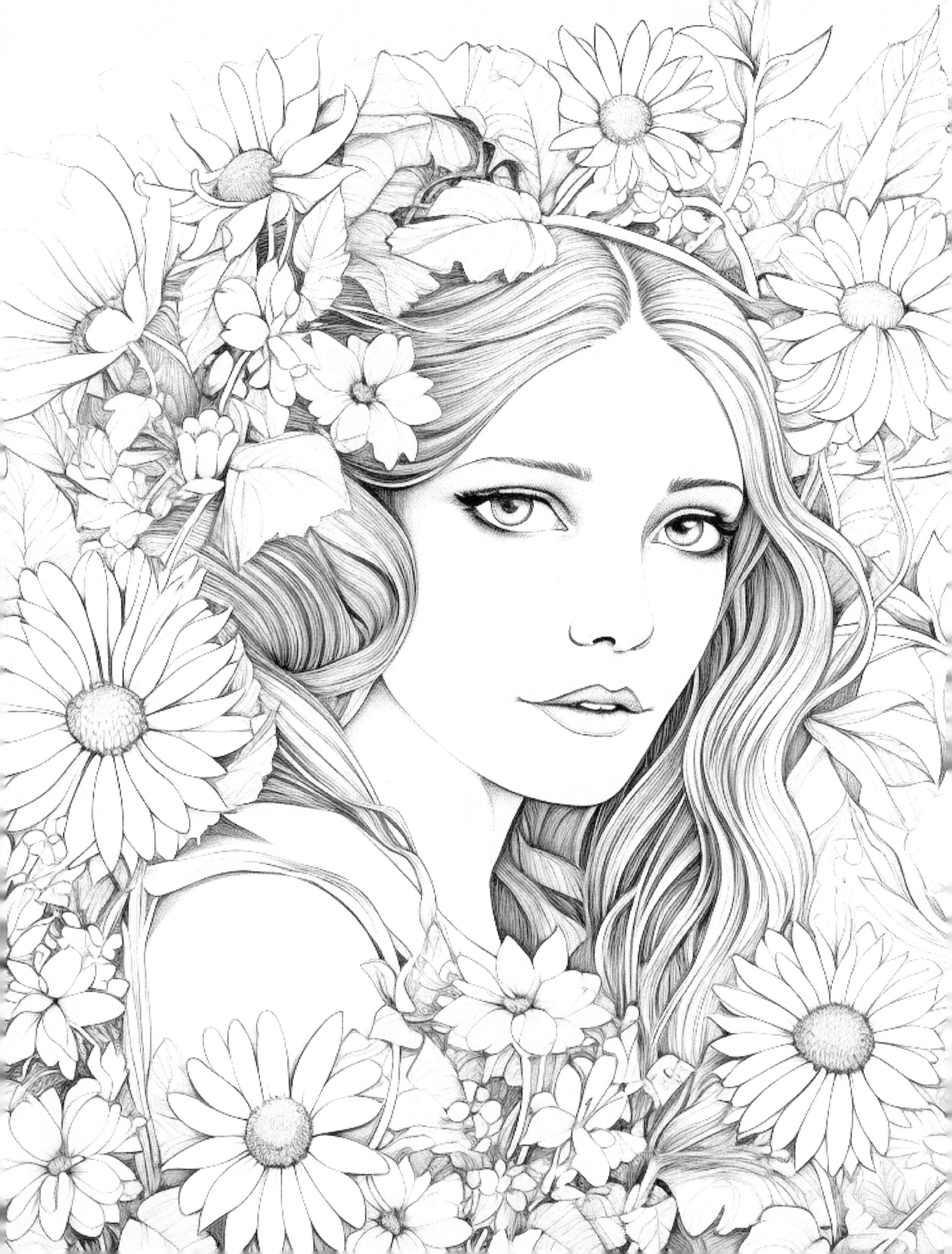

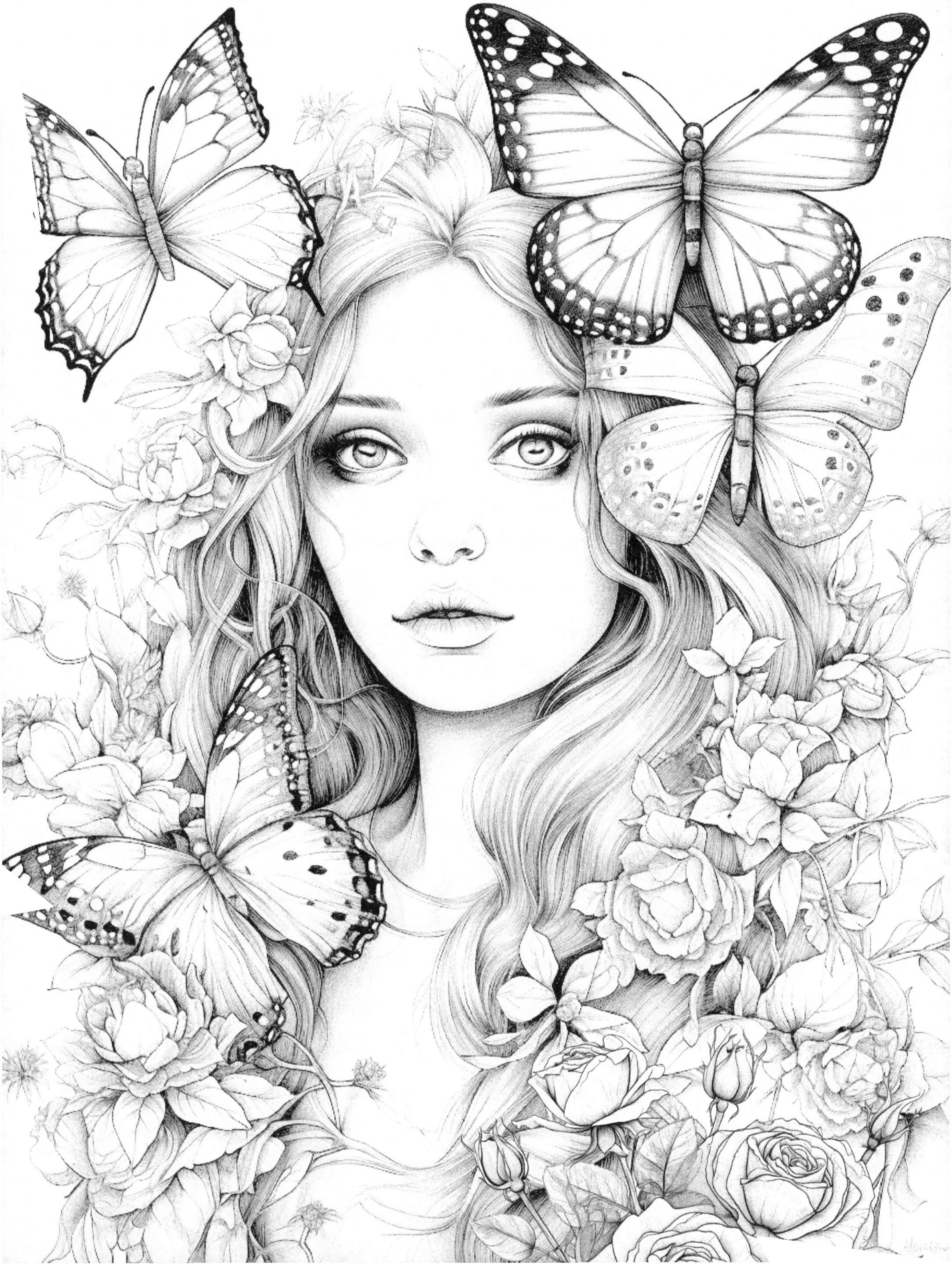

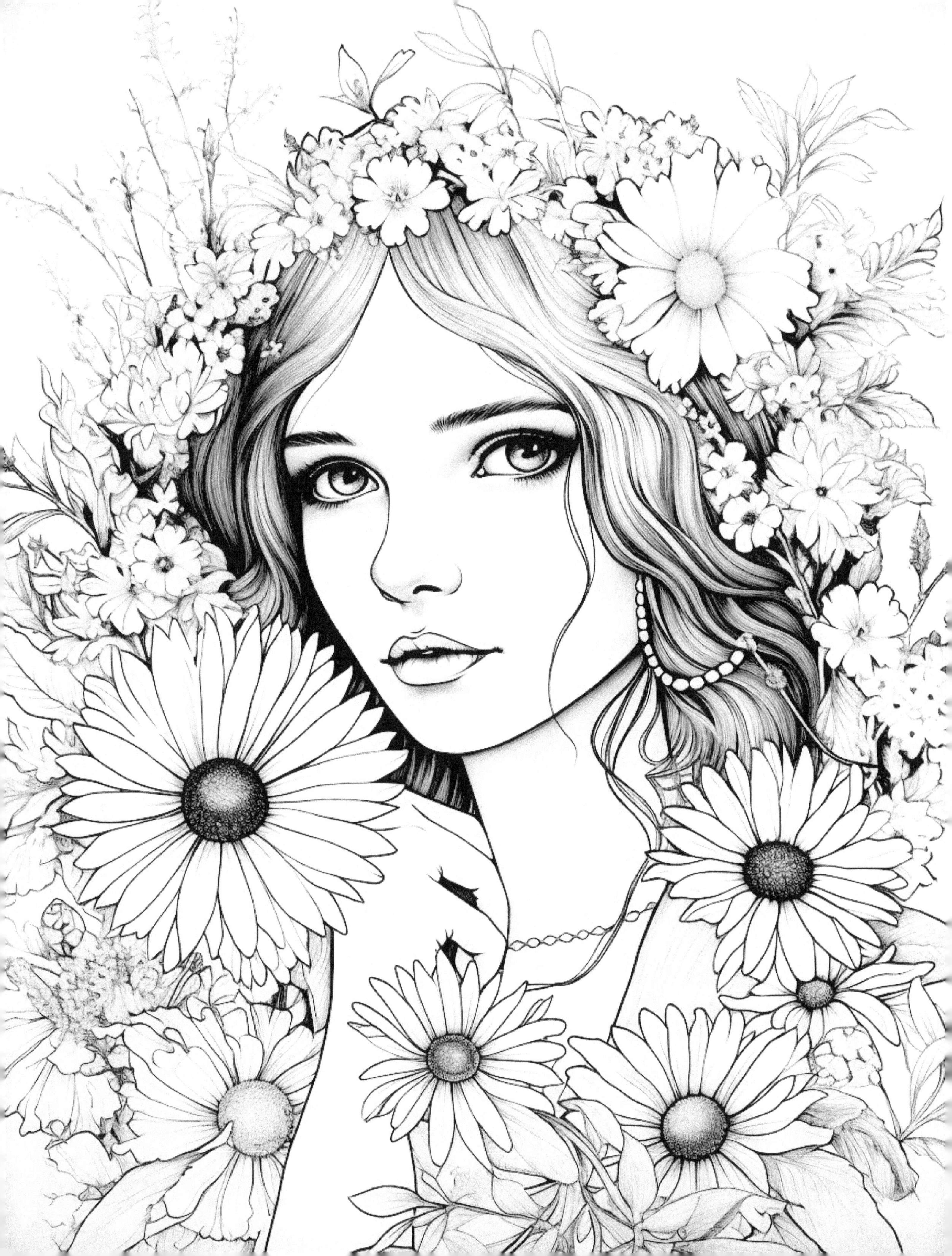

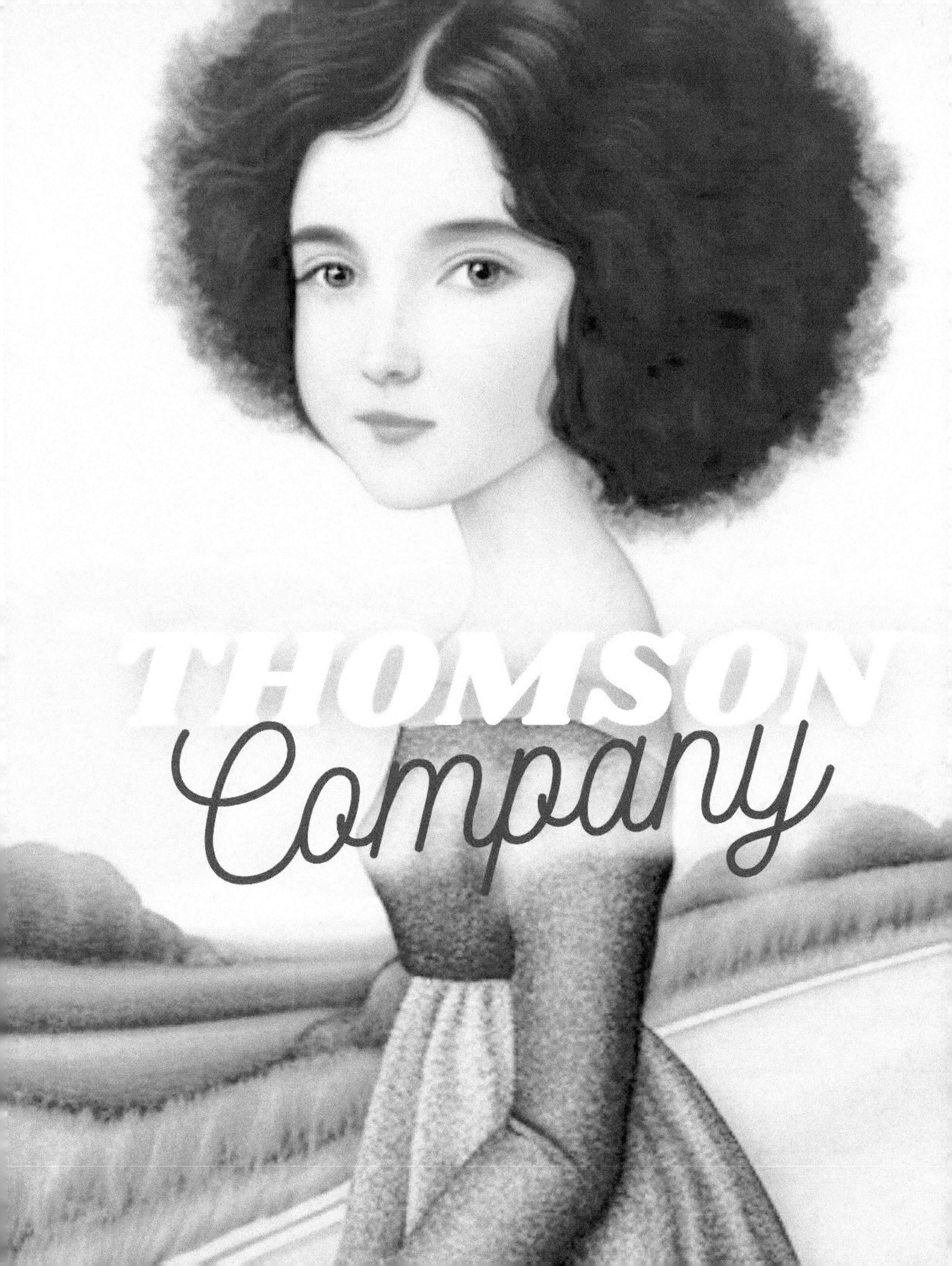
THOMSON
Company

www.ingramcontent.com/pod-product-compliance
Lightning Source LLC
Chambersburg PA
CBHW080547220526
45466CB00010B/3067
* 9 7 9 8 3 9 4 4 9 0 8 2 8 *